Grow your
own Achievers

Communicators is an imprint of How To Books.
For further details please send for a free copy of the latest catalogue
3 Newtec Place, Magdalen Road, Oxford OX4 1RE United Kingdom

Grow your
own Achievers

A manager's guide to
developing effective people

Lesley Morrissey

communicators

Published by How To Books Ltd,
3 Newtec Place, Magdalen Road,
Oxford OX4 1RE. United Kingdom.
Tel: (01865) 793806. Fax: (01865) 248780
e-mail: info@howtobooks.co.uk
http://www.howtobooks.co.uk

First edition 2002

British Library Cataloguing in Publication Data.
A catalogue record for this book is available from the British Library.

Edited by Francesca Mitchell
Cover design by Baseline Arts Ltd, Oxford

Produced for How To Books by Deer Park Productions
Typeset by PDQ Typesetting, Newcastle-under-Lyme, Staffordshire
Printed and bound in Great Britain by Bell & Bain Ltd, Glasgow

NOTE: The material contained in this book is set out in good faith for general
guidance and no liability can be accepted for loss or expense incurred as a
result of relying in particular circumstances on statements made in this book.
Laws and regulations are complex and liable to change, and readers should
check the current position with the relevant authorities before making
personal arrangements.

Communicators is an imprint of How To Books.

Contents

their own objectives to create an ongoing environment
of achievement.

9 Goals, Aims and Objectives 95

People don't come to work to achieve the company's
goals. What they do at work is the means of generating
either money, power or prestige which will affect them
personally outside work. Work is what they do to
achieve their personal goals. Understand personal goals
to help to focus on work goals.

10 Priorities and Action Plans 103

Explains the process of setting goals. Examines the
various goals individuals have and a means of
prioritizing them. Understand the difference between
a goal and an action. Develop action plans that work.

Part 4 – How to Make Training Really Work

11 Training 110

Explore various means of helping staff to learn new
skills, new knowledge and change methods to improve
effectiveness. Examine the need for training – how else
can a result be achieved? Looks at monitoring
development and planning time frames.

12 Preparing for Improvement 122

Involve staff in their own development. Discuss why
change needs to take place, what outcomes are
expected and the means of achieving these. Help staff
to set their own measurable objectives so they know
when they have been achieved. Discusses processes to
gain agreement and ownership of the results.

13 After the Event . . . 132

When development has been achieved, how to bridge the gap between theory and practice. Discusses the development experience, what needs to be established and how to use collaborative means to do this. How to be an active ingredient in your staff's success, what you have to do – and what not to do!

Part 5 – How to Get Promoted

14 What Next? 139

Explore what happens when the result you wanted has been achieved. Revisit development strategies to improve another aspect of performance. Ensure that you use the same processes you are asking your staff to use. How to ensure that, when your staff are good enough to take over your job, you are ready to move on up!

Preface

Every manager dreams of managing a high performing team. Unfortunately, the manager who is lucky enough to manage such a team is a rare individual.

Much more common are the managers who complain: 'Why don't my staff work as they are supposed to?' So what is the secret of getting a high performing team – is it luck or is it hard work and good management?

The answers are in the following pages. It's not rocket science; these techniques are good common sense and work for anyone who wants them to. It doesn't matter where you are in the hierarchy – whether you've just made supervisor or are a senior manager with managers reporting to you. They work for human beings.

The techniques don't provide a quick fix; they require a certain amount of time and effort. However, on the bonus side, they take less and less effort the longer you use them.

They are good management practices and contribute to such strategies as Investors in People (IiP) and ISO 9000/1/2, as well as helping the individuals involved to gain their own qualifications, such as NVQs, City & Guilds certificates and professional qualifications.

Staff managed with these techniques have higher levels of job satisfaction, and are more creative, innovative, dedicated, optimistic, energetic and enthusiastic. Managers who use these techniques are successful, high performers who get promoted and gain the respect and admiration of their peers and superiors.

What are the drawbacks?

If other managers don't use these techniques, your department may feel they have to operate on two levels, as they will find other departments may not co-operate with their preferred way of working. However, with the right input, staff will continue to perform for you and for themselves.

If senior managers don't 'buy' your methods, you may have to deal with a certain amount of negative input. However, in most companies, senior managers are usually delighted with anything that gets higher levels of performance. If you do your preparation properly you will be able to point to the bottom line with confidence, showing that your team's efforts have improved it.

So – you get a high performing team, you get promoted, and you can directly affect the company's profit line – what are you waiting for?

Lesley Morrissey

Lesley can be contacted at:
The Attitudes & Inside News Partnership
27 Maltings Road
Great Baddow
Chelmsford, Essex CM2 8HQ
Telefax: 01245 475111
Email: attitudes@blueyonder.co.uk
Or insidenews@blueyonder.co.uk

Chapter 1

How can you GROW an Achiever?

In this Chapter:

- ◆ **recognizing negative attitudes and their effects**
- ◆ **using your attitude to influence others**
- ◆ **the secret of a positive attitude and how it is created**
- ◆ **the impact of being positive.**

Some people in your team may already achieve well and, possibly, quite consistently. However, there are bound to be some who never seem to get out of first gear.

Why aren't they achieving now?

The first step along the way to turning your team into high performers is to look at each individual. Would you describe them as positive or negative in their approach? Do you hear words or phrases such as:

> 'We can't do that.'
> 'That won't work.'
> 'It isn't worth it.'
> 'There's no point in doing that.'
> 'Nobody notices what we do anyway.'
> 'It doesn't matter.'

'I don't care.'

'*They* don't care.'

'We'll never get that done in time.'

'I'll do my best.'

'I'll try.'

'I'll see what I can do.'

'I haven't got time.'

'We never seem to get to the end of this.'

'*They* expect miracles from us, we're not superhuman.'

The language that people use indicates the way in which they think. People who use negatives such as 'not', 'can't', 'won't', 'don't', 'haven't' are the sort of people who see challenges as problems and give up easily.

People are often quick to blame others – '*they*' can always be held responsible. '*They*' are usually 'the management'. This is just another way of people in your team not taking responsibility for their own actions.

Recognizing negative attitudes

People who use words like 'try', 'I'll see' and even 'I'll do my best' are telling you that they haven't decided to succeed. They probably don't think it's possible, but they know you are expecting a positive response. Listen to the tone of voice – it usually tells you far more than the words.

How many times have you heard someone say 'I'll do my best' and known that they have no intention of doing their best? In fact, they probably have no idea what their best is – they have never tested themselves to the limit.

People with negative approaches are not necessarily depressives who cast doom and gloom over everyone they meet. Most of them function quite adequately and their negative attitudes go unnoticed in the work place.

Attitudes are contagious – is yours worth catching?

Think about your own attitude. You will have absolutely no chance of influencing your team if you are Mr or Ms Negative yourself. You were not born with a negative approach, any more than anybody in your team was. Your attitude is the result of many years of programming and experience – but it doesn't have to stay that way.

Developing a positive approach is something you can choose to do. Your current attitude is the result of *other people's* programming. Why let others decide your attitude? Take control and choose to be positive. It will take work and there will be days when you find it hard to maintain, but if you really want to become an achiever yourself, stick with it.

Chapter 2 and Chapter 3 will show you how to develop a positive approach and the tools to maintain it. Practise these first on yourself until you have successfully got to the point where you don't have to think about how you do things and how you say things. At this point you can start using them to help your team to develop.

A word of advice – you can help your team get there much more quickly if you act as 'programmer' and support. If you want to get there more quickly yourself, you may need a mentor or partner to help you over the tough patches.

What is positive attitude anyway?

On the surface it is the way you communicate your mood to others. When you are optimistic and anticipate successful outcomes and encounters, you transmit a positive attitude and people usually respond favourably. You only visualize success and, therefore, reduce the likelihood of failure. Problems and obstacles are seen only as challenges to be overcome.

When you are pessimistic and expect the worst, your attitude is often negative, and people tend to avoid you. You are looking for obstacles and problems to stop you – and if you look hard enough you are sure to find what you are looking for!

Attitude is never static – it is an ongoing dynamic, sensitive, perceptual process. Unless you are on constant guard, negative factors can slip into your perspective which will cause you to spend time on obstacles rather than opportunities.

Why are people negative more often than positive?

If you are around negative factors for long enough, they will be reflected in your attitude. The negative overshadows the positive. Most human beings focus on negative outcomes and effects, so it's hardly surprising that people 'infect' each other with negative 'vibes'. It's a challenge to reject the negative factors – those who learn the 'trick' will reflect it and others will notice.

What is the secret of 'getting' a positive attitude?

No one can be positive all the time – excessive optimism is not realistic. Positive attitude is not an act; it must be genuine. When things are going well, a positive attitude becomes self-perpetuating and easy to maintain. There is always something that will challenge your ability to bounce back – winners are those who can regain their positive attitudes quickly.

> It doesn't matter how many times you fall down. It's the number of times you get back up that counts.

When something turns your mental focus in a negative direction, positive people know that a positive attitude is a state of mind that can be maintained only through conscious effort.

Does it matter if your staff are negative?

This depends on how interested you are in getting high levels of results from your staff. Positive people get better results more quickly than negative people. When difficulties occur, negative people will spend a great deal of their time explaining why a certain outcome is not possible. Positive people look at what has to be done to overcome the problem.

Positive people have more energy and much more enthusiasm than negative people. Being positive helps your mind to think freely. Ideas and solutions rise to the surface. A negative attitude, on the other hand, has a stifling effect and creativity is suffocated.

What is the difference?

When it comes to your staff, positive people get results; negative people tell you why they can't get the results you want.

Your positive approach rubs off on your team and encourages similar behaviour. Negative behaviour influences those around you and gives rise to negative expectations – which would you prefer?

The sales pitch – what's in it for ME?

Your ability to keep your own attitude positive will ensure:

- you see challenges to be overcome and not problems which stop you achieving
- your success rate will improve
- other people will notice the results.

I'm sure you can think of many more benefits – some will be very specific to you and your particular situation. It's worth writing these down to remind yourself of why you should stick at it.

If you can influence your team to be more positive:

- they will save you time trying to solve their problems as they will start to think of solutions for themselves
- they will be more enthusiastic and energetic about their work
- they will be happier and easier to be around
- they will get more out of their jobs in the way of satisfaction.

There are other benefits that you and your team will experience if you make the effort. Get people to think about what the outcomes will be for them to help to keep them on track.

Remember, everyone is different and what will make one person keen to work, may not do anything for somebody else. Ensure everyone thinks about themselves and how positive outcomes will get them what *they* want.

Reflection points

Think of the most negative person you know.

◆ How do you feel about this person?
◆ What is your emotional reaction to their verbal comments about things that are happening in their life or at work?
◆ How would you feel if you overheard someone describing you like this to another person?

Think of someone you know personally who has a very positive approach to life.

◆ What is it about them that makes them positive?
◆ Think about the words you would use to describe this person to someone who had never met them.
◆ How would you feel if someone described you like this?

Action points

Ask your staff to complete the following questionnaire.

Give yourself marks out of ten for the following – 1 is low, 10 is high (the best you can be).

1.   Based on our communication over the past month, my boss would give me_____out of ten for positive approach.

2. My co-workers would rate my attitude as____.
3. Realistically, I would rate my current attitude as____.
4. In dealing with other people, I would score the effect of my attitude as a____.
5. My current creativity level, based on my approach to problems and difficulties, is____.
6. If there were a meter that could gauge my sense of humour I believe it would read____.
7. The patience and sensitivity I have shown others recently deserves a rating of____.
8. When it comes to not allowing little things to bother me, I deserve____.
9. Based upon the number of compliments I have received lately, I deserve____.
10. I would rate my enthusiasm towards my job during the past few weeks as____.

◆ A score of 90 or over is a sign that your attitude is 'in tune'.
◆ A score of 70-90 indicates that minor adjustments may be required.
◆ A rating between 50-70 suggests that a major change is needed.
◆ If you rated yourself below 50 a complete overhaul is suggested.

Do the same exercise for yourself and assess how each of your staff will rate themselves – before you see their results.

◆ How close were your assessments of their scores to their own?

◆ Where do you disagree with their self-assessment?

◆ Talk to them about it and discuss what steps could be taken, by you and by them, to improve things.

Chapter 2

Accentuate the POSITIVE

In this Chapter:

◆ **working on the positive aspects**

◆ **positive approaches and their impact on results**

◆ **how your subconscious works**

◆ **the link between habits and attitudes**

◆ **the belief system and how to use it to get results.**

The power of the positive

Lots of people have heard of PMA – Positive Mental Attitude. Many people think it is something you are born with or that it is the outcome of a life that has been untroubled by crises and disasters. If you know anyone who has sailed through life without any kind of ripple, I'll show you someone who has no idea how to achieve success and will come unstuck at the first sign of a challenge!

Attitude is something you choose – certainly not something you are born with. However, the reality is that some days go better than others.

◆ 'Good' days produce good feelings and you seem to get much more done.

◆ 'Bad' days tend to turn into 'one of those days' and
   things go wrong one after another.

People who learn to use a positive approach rarely have
a day that they could describe as 'one of those days' –
unless it is in terms of yet another of those fantastic days
where everything goes right and they achieve great
results!

Most people think in negative terms for around 80% of
the time – overcoming this is a real challenge. Negative
thoughts attract more negative thoughts. Unless you
make an effort to break out of the negative train of
thought, you will go down the spiral and spend most of
your time feeling unhappy with your life.

The opposite is also true. Positive thoughts attract more
positive thoughts. If you make the effort to think in
positive terms, you will go up the spiral and the result
will be a fruitful and satisfying life.

How your mind works

Let's take a look at how your mind works. You operate
on two levels:

◆ conscious – the part of your mind that operates
   deliberately with thought
◆ subconscious – the part of your mind that carries out
   commands unconsciously, your 'automatic pilot'.

When we first start to learn something, we use the conscious part of our mind and back the experience up with previous knowledge from the subconscious. If we have never tackled a task before, the conscious mind will be concentrating on the actions whilst the subconscious is either trying to defeat you or spurring you on, depending on your attitude.

Case study

When you first learn to write, you learn with your conscious mind. Everything is awkward, you have to think about every little movement of your pencil and your hand. Each line or curve has to be carefully controlled and made in the right direction. It seems impossible to produce straight lines and smooth curves, let alone produce a letter which sits on the line.

As the lessons progress, the tiny actions start to become habit. Now you write without thinking about how the letters are formed – they just appear.

Imagine you hadn't learned to write until you were an adult. The thought of learning to write would now have become a major obstacle. You may have tried a few times and failed, and the subconscious would make you relive the failure and keep reminding you that writing wasn't for you. You could be influenced by outsiders or just by your own fears, but it is the subconscious that stops you.

Once we realize this, we can control the power of the mind and, therefore, it is our choice whether we use it constructively or destructively.

The subconscious part of your mind is actually the most powerful, and the average human only uses less than one percent of their mind's capability. The subconscious only reacts to what you feed it; it doesn't have the ability to know what is good or bad for you.

◆ Feed your subconscious mind with positive messages and the conscious mind will produce positive actions.
◆ You are who you think you are.
◆ Your subconscious mind is working right now, day and night, to make sure that you become precisely the person you unconsciously believe yourself to be.

Habits and attitudes

Habits are actions we repeat over and over again, without thinking much about them. They are learned responses. We all have them – good ones and bad ones. The area in your brain that 'remembers' your habits doesn't make judgements about whether a habit is good or bad – as long as you do something often enough, it becomes a habit and slips from conscious activity to subconscious activity.

Driving is a habit. When you first learn to drive, all your thoughts are very conscious. You have to think about when to take your hand off the wheel to change gear, when to look in the mirror, when to take your foot off the accelerator or hit the brake. It is uncomfortable – because you have to *think* about it consciously.

However, when you have passed your driving test and have been driving for a while, you may think about what is going on outside the car, but little conscious thought goes into the operation of the vehicle. It has become a habit – or subconscious activity.

Trying to persuade someone to change a habit is difficult – because they now have to remember to think about it every time they do it. It's easier to do it the way they have learned – so changing habits is resisted, usually quite strongly.

Belief systems

We all have a belief system, but everyone has differing beliefs. In Chapter 3 we'll be looking at where our beliefs come from, but for now we'll look at how they affect our actions.

Examples

If you were brought up in a family that had several members who regularly committed crimes – such as burglary or car theft – you might know on a conscious level that this is wrong, but your attitude is quite likely to be accommodating to this sort of activity. If someone asked you to do something dishonest you might find it easy to agree.

If you were brought up in a family where servants were always there to look after you, you might not realize that it is not acceptable to leave clothes out for someone else to put away in other people's homes. If you visit friends who do not have servants, it might not occur to you to tidy up your clothes.

When there is an outbreak of flu in an office, people catch it one after another. You will hear people saying 'I think I'm getting the flu,' and, sure enough, a day or two later they are off sick.

But if a family has several members sick with flu, how often is the mother struck down? Think back to your childhood; look at large families that you know. It seems to go through the family but Mum doesn't usually get it – or, if she does, she gets a mild dose after everyone else is better and back at work and school. This is not because mothers have a different immune system to the rest of us. It's because they cannot afford to be ill. A subconscious trigger will tell them 'I cannot become sick, or nobody would be there to look after the family'. They believe they must remain healthy and, mostly, they do.

The mind is powerful – you just need to know how to program in the messages that get this kind of result.

How to believe

This might sound nonsensical – you either believe or you don't – you can't make yourself believe something.

On one level this is true – you won't believe something you *know* and can *prove* to be untrue. Neither will you believe something that goes against your essential moral values. However, you don't necessarily have to believe something to be true to achieve it.

Case study

You may have heard of Morris Goodman. He is an American who, in March 1981 was flying a light aircraft, hit some overhead wires on the way in to land and crashed. He lived, but suffered many injuries:

◆ His spine had been crushed, severely damaging his central nervous system.
◆ He had broken C1 and C2 – the first two vertebrae that attach the neck to the head (at this time nobody had survived after breaking these).
◆ His larynx had been crushed, making speaking impossible and making it difficult for him to swallow.
◆ The nerves to his diaphragm were severed, so he was unable to push his lungs up and down and needed a respirator to breathe.

The prognosis was that, with an operation, and long-term hospitalization, he might be able to sit in a wheelchair unaided in about 20 months' time. Morris believed that he would walk out of the hospital in six months! He continued to imagine himself doing all the things that 'normal' people do every day, and just before Christmas 1981 he left the hospital, upright, breathing unaided, able to speak and to eat, on his own two feet. At one point one of his doctors asked him, 'What are your long term expectations?' He replied, 'I expect to be able to function normally.' The doctor warned him, 'You will never function as a normal man again.' Morris's reply: 'I don't care if you believe that, but if I do I'm going to be in trouble!'

Belief gets results

When I was studying for my professional qualifications, I was struggling with one of the subjects – managing information systems. This encompassed management information systems, statistics and accounts. Consider that my father did most of my maths homework when I was at school and I had a strong belief that I could not add up, let alone do complex equations, and you might understand why I was having a problem!

I went to a positive attitude seminar and, at the end, asked the speaker how I could improve my chances of passing my exams in less than a month. She advised me to keep telling myself I could.

I quickly responded, 'But I'm no good with numbers.'

'As long as you keep telling yourself that, it will be true.'

'So what can I do?' I asked, puzzled by this.

'Keep telling yourself "I'm really good with numbers" – every time you hear yourself think or say "I'm no good with numbers", change it – say it out loud if necessary,' she said.

'But I don't believe that. It's not true,' I argued.

'Don't worry, belief will kick in if you say it often enough,' she assured me.

What was the outcome? I tried it – every time I heard that internal voice saying 'Don't be silly, you can't add up', I said out loud 'I'm really good with numbers.'

I passed the exam – with higher marks than any of the others! The belief had kicked in and broken down the mental block that prevented me taking in the information I needed to succeed.

The sales pitch – what's in it for ME?

As a manager, being positive, learning good habits and using your belief system will:

◆ ensure you have more energy – and create more energy in your team
◆ improve your time management – you'll get more done in less time
◆ reduce barriers to success by concentrating only on what *can* be achieved

- improve your daily routine by learning more effective methods of doing those day-to-day tasks
- reduce time wasted in avoiding doing jobs you dislike.

It will also do all this for your team if you encourage them to practise these skills.

Reflection points

Think about a time when you were very successful in a particular task.

- How did you feel?
- What did you say to yourself?
- What did other people say to you?
- What effect did this have on your work rate?

Think about a time when you had great difficulties with a particular task and failed to achieve the expected outcome.

- How did you feel?
- What did you say to yourself?
- What did other people say to you?
- How did other people act around you?
- What effect did this have on your willingness to work?

Action points

Take a plain piece of paper.

- ◆ Write your name as you normally sign it.
- ◆ Now write your name backwards – from right to left.
- ◆ Now try to write your name with the other hand.

- ◆ How long did the first signature take?
- ◆ How long did the second one take?
- ◆ What about the third one?
- ◆ How do the three signatures compare?

Unless you have had experience in writing with the 'wrong' hand, it is almost certain that you will have difficulty in producing neat writing at a comparable speed to that you can produce with the 'right' hand. There is no physiological reason you cannot write effectively with either hand. It is all to do with learning the habit and belief that you can do it. Once you have reached the 'automatic' level of writing, you are using your subconscious mind. The subconscious is the very thing that allows you to learn to write 'without thinking'.

Subconscious habits and beliefs can be changed, but it takes effort.

Chapter 3

Programming

In this Chapter:

- **the chain of programming that gets results**
- **how beliefs are created**
- **programming ourselves and others**
- **guarding against negative expectations.**

What we want is results

We're all looking for results – more often than not, *how* we do the job isn't important, what *is* important is the result.

- **Results** only happen if you take the actions that produce them.

- Logical as this may seem, the **actions** that you take are almost infinitely variable depending on all sorts of other factors, such as how much other work you have to accomplish, what sort of day you've had so far, whether your colleagues are helpful or a pain in the neck and how clearly you can see the point of doing whatever it is you have to do.

- The **feelings** that you have about all these issues will dictate whether you get 'stuck in' with enthusiasm or whether you do as little as possible to get a result that just about meets the requirements.

◆ The feelings are created by your **attitudes** – whether you approach work from a 'whatever it takes to get the best possible result' or 'I hate work and I'll only do what I have to' angle.

◆ Your **beliefs** will create these attitudes. Imagine that you believed all managers were idiots or power crazy – what sort of effect would that have on your willingness to help them to get the results they wanted? How about if your manager was your best friend outside work – your belief that they were a good person that you liked would make you want to give them every scrap of help you could, wouldn't it?

◆ Beliefs come from the **programming** you have received over the years. This might be beliefs that were passed on from your parents and other family members. It might be from previous experiences you have had with the way that other managers have behaved, or from experiences related to you by friends.

If you follow the chain of programming that produces the results you get, it looks like this:

Programming → Beliefs → Attitudes → Feelings → Actions → Results

If this is how the brain works and we want to learn to change the results we are currently obtaining in life, we must start at the beginning of the chain – programming.

The source of programming

How do we acquire programming? In the first instance, you are programmed consciously or, more often, unconsciously, by the people around you. As a child, these people were your family, friends and playmates.

Parents programme children to succeed – and sometimes to fail. Consider a child bringing home a report card from school. English has high marks, but the maths assessment indicates that there is room for improvement. A caring parent wants to congratulate his child on doing well in English and perhaps reassure the child that he is not angry at the maths assessment.

'Don't worry, you got good marks in English – and you can't be good at everything.'

This sort of phrase is commonly heard about many different skills. Unfortunately, although the intentions are good, the parent is programming the child to be poor at maths. Before long the child will be saying to his friends 'I'm no good at maths,' because he has heard someone else tell him he is not good at it. How many adults do you know who will happily announce, 'Don't ask me to work the bill out, I can't add up.' Over a long period of time, these people have programmed themselves to be poor at figures. Constant repetition has reinforced this idea.

The truth? We all have the capacity to do far more mentally than we do. There are people who can manipulate numbers and produce instant answers to calculations that would require ten minutes with a calculator for most of us. We might argue that we could not do this, but the ability is there for all of us – we just don't use it. Usually, because someone has told us it isn't possible often enough, we end up believing it.

Negative messages

We programme ourselves. We repeat messages to ourselves both silently and out loud. How many times have you heard someone close to you repeat a particular message about their skills? For instance:

'I can't add up.'
'I don't understand computers.'
'I can't spell for toffee.'
'I'm useless with anything technical.'
'I always have to get my son to programme the video.'
'I'm no good with people.'
'I'm terrified of standing up to speak in front of a group.'
'I'm always late.'

You will almost certainly have your own 'negative programme' that you run regularly.

What happens when you say these things? Do you have a mental picture of yourself doing whatever it is and being successful? No. It's more likely that you keep seeing yourself *not* doing it, so what you are actually doing is feeding into your internal computer continual pictures of failure.

The interesting fact to consider is that the central nervous system cannot tell the difference between a real event and an imagined event, providing the imagined event is in clear detail and is repeated often enough to programme the subconscious to 'see' that as reality.

Now consider why you might want to change your programming to something positive, rather than keep repeating negative messages.

Self-fulfilling prophecies

If you have ever heard the phrase 'a self-fulfilling prophecy', this is precisely what we are talking about. All this means is that once you have stated that a particular course of action is likely to produce a specific result, you tend to start behaving as though this is a foregone conclusion. In other words, you get what you expect.

Do you *want* to fail at anything? Most of us don't, but we don't get any support to try to overcome our weaker areas. We hear ourselves stating that we cannot do something (see above list) and other people are listening, have no reason to discourage us from this belief and, consequently, behave as though this were true.

This is also known as a limiting belief. We do it to ourselves.

Programming from other people

Sometimes other people do it to us. We hear a lot of negative messages from others about our skills, knowledge, capabilities, aptitudes and behaviours. If we choose to accept them we start behaving as though these were true. We *can* choose to reject these messages and take action to ensure they are not true.

For instance, 'Don't give Sue anything that needs to be accurate, she's hopeless at details.' If you were Sue, how would you feel about this type of statement? You might prefer to be seen as being a reliable person who pays attention to details. If you accept the message you will start to ignore details – because everyone expects you to be hopeless. If you reject the message you will take extra care and, soon, people will forget the occasion when you were less accurate and only remember the many occasions when you produced good results.

As a manager this means that you must not only be conscious of the messages you give yourself and accept from others, but you must also be very careful not to programme your staff with limiting messages that will produce work of a lesser quality.

Programming is powerful – you can use it to feed positive messages to your team.

Check your language. How much of what you say to your team and about your team is positive? Are you programming people to fail? Try changing your focus and using language that gives people positive messages about what they *can* do, not negative messages about the likelihood of failure. People may not be aware of a change, or, if they are, they will not know what has changed.

Attitude and motivation

Real achievers don't accept other people's view of things – they decide what is possible and then make it happen. Positive attitude is purely a belief that there is a way to do whatever you want – if you want it badly enough. Some people call this motivation.

What most people *don't* understand, is that the more focused and positive you are, the higher levels of motivation you will have. Negative people tend towards lethargy and 'can't be bothered'. Positive people have some mysterious source of energy and creativity that they are always able to tap into.

The sales pitch – what's in it for ME?

As a manager:

◆ You will find yourself able to achieve more if you programme yourself positively.

- Other people – your team, your boss and your colleagues – will change their perception of your achievement levels just by listening to the way you speak.
- You will get better quality results from the people who work for you.
- You will be able to record how success has been achieved, and, therefore, repeat it.
- Some of your staff will surprise you with their achievements – most people don't know how much they can do themselves!
- You will surprise yourself by finding jobs easier and less trouble to complete.
- You will become known as a manager who gets results.
- You may even become known as a manager who can work miracles!

If you understand how your team accept programming:

- You can ensure they get positive programming from you.
- You can help them to understand the unconscious process and develop a more positive approach.
- You will be able to reinforce successes with positive feedback.
- They will get less negative input.

◆ You can help them to recognize and reject negative messages and improve their success rate.

Reflection points

◆ How much less stress would you experience if your team got on with things without complaining or talking about all the reasons why it won't work?

◆ What would happen if your team were always focused on successful outcomes and had a clear idea of how they will achieve them?

◆ What sort of atmosphere would you have in the office if everyone was focused on success?

◆ What would this do for productivity, absenteeism and team spirit?

Action points

Choose one person who would benefit from a more positive approach.

◆ **Talk to them about their job and only discuss the things that they do well. If they raise any negative points tell them, 'I know there have been challenges, but I know you are more than able to overcome these. I have every confidence in your ability to succeed.' You can use your own words, but they should convey this positive message.**

- Keep supporting them by telling them how well they are doing. Look for small successes and tell them you've noticed and how pleased you are. Don't overdo it and don't be insincere, look for genuine reasons for praise.
- After one week assess whether this person has improved their attitude, approach and performance at all.
- Assess again after two weeks and then after one month. You will be surprised at the difference.

Chapter 4

The Company

In this Chapter:

- ◆ **understanding where you are going**
- ◆ **establishing the objectives**
- ◆ **making a departmental contribution**
- ◆ **company culture**
- ◆ **outlining how your staff can contribute**
- ◆ **getting focused.**

Where are we going?

Now you're operating in positive mode, the next step is to get your staff focused on achieving the business goals. If you are one of the many managers who fall into the following categories, you may need to take another course of action first.

- ◆ Nobody has told you what the business goals are.
- ◆ As far as you know the business doesn't have any goals.
- ◆ The business goals change weekly.

How can I find out?

If you don't know, or are unsure of, what the business goals are, the only way to find out is to ask. Ask the person at the top, if possible. If this isn't possible, ask the nearest person to the person at the top you can get to.

If you're not sure how to tackle this, try the following approach:

> 'I'm getting my team focused on useful results and it would be helpful if we could prioritize our work in relation to the things which are most important to the company. Can you give me a copy of the mission statement (or corporate objectives or business goals) or just give me a brief run down on the key issues for our company?'

If no such things as business objectives exist, look at what the company has done so far. To really find out what you need to know, you should embark on some serious question asking – of others and of yourself. In many instances you may need to do some research to uncover the real answers to these questions. Below is a list of areas and questions that will help you to establish the focus for your company, whether you work for a multinational, a micro-business or something in between.

What sort of markets are we in?

- Are we upper, middle or lower end of the market?
- What sort of products or services do we supply?
- Are we tightly focused on a very small range of products and services, or very diverse with many products and services?
- Do we win price battles with competitors at any cost or is quality more important than getting into a price war?
- Is our focus local, national or international?

Who are our competitors?

These may be different for different product ranges or service types if your company is very diverse. Everyone in your business is not a competitor – for instance, Sainsbury's competes with Tesco, but although they offer some similar products, neither of them really compete directly with Fortnum and Mason or Harrods Food Hall. However, Sainsbury's and Tesco may also overlap in services with small independent grocery stores, with high street banks and loan companies, with petrol stations and with local fruit and vegetable markets.

What are they trying to achieve?

If you can identify what your competitors are trying to achieve, you should have a reasonable idea of what your own company is aiming for. The goals are likely to be similar. Don't jump to the obvious conclusions or write the competition off without careful thought.

What is the approach to products or services offered?

◆ Is each product/service carefully thought through and planned with appropriate market research?

◆ Does the company produce a product/service and then create a market for it or find a market need that is not being filled and fill it?

◆ Is the product development proactive or reactive – in other words, do they invent their own new products or try to improve on somebody else's idea?

◆ Are there clear quality standards and monitoring processes?

◆ How strongly do the top management believe in the company's products/services?

It doesn't matter if your company is relatively small, you can still examine these issues to help you to be focused.

What is the company's attitude towards their customers?

◆ Does the company do anything that makes customers unhappy?

◆ What does the company do to satisfy unhappy customers?

◆ How much does the company value its customers? What level of effort will be made to meet customer needs – is it 'whatever it takes' or 'we'll sort it out eventually'?

- Does the organization take customers into account when planning for the future or are they an afterthought?

What is the attitude towards the staff?

- What sort of programmes for staff development are there?
- Are there regular salary reviews in relation to both cost of living and merit/performance issues?
- Are salaries always paid on time?
- Are health care, pension arrangements or other benefits and facilities available?
- What is the attitude when a key member of staff moves on – leaving parties and gifts or are they treated as an 'ungrateful individual leaving us in the lurch'?

What sort of operating policies are in place?

- Does the company promote from within or bring in fresh blood from outside?
- Do departments communicate freely and work together or is there a competitive attitude based on 'points scoring' between departments?
- Does the managing director or chief executive have an open door policy or can they be seen by appointment only?

◆ If your company has more than 100 staff, how well do you know them all – would you recognize most of them if you bumped into them in the street (and would the chief executive know them)?

What issues are most important to the managing director?

◆ Is their position and status something they protect?
◆ Are they a hands on or hands off manager?
◆ Do they delegate or tend to do things themselves?
◆ Do they feel the need to be 'kept in the picture' all the time?
◆ Do they like seeing their picture in the newspaper or business publications?
◆ Do they enjoy addressing the 'troops'?
◆ What is their pet subject, i.e. are they a financial wizard, a marketing expert, a purchasing genius, etc.?
◆ What are their personal strengths – political manoeuvring, entrepreneurial approach, getting people to do what they want, public relations, risk taking, being 'of the people', generating personal loyalty, etc.?

What sort of company culture is in operation?

◆ Are the systems the key to everything? In other words, do the systems work for you or do you work for the systems?

- Is innovation and creativity encouraged or is everything done 'by the book'?
- How much interaction between departments is there? Is it all at manager level, or do staff at all levels communicate interdepartmentally?
- How much information flows down from the top? How much flows to the top?
- Is the company a rumour factory or is everything open and information freely available to all?
- When major moves are on the agenda – product launches, redundancy, mergers, new premises, new equipment, changes in direction – at what point are the staff informed?
  - Are they told early on, once the plans are clear and work needs to be started?

  or

  - Are only those who need to know told and everyone else finds out when there is no way to keep it from them any longer?
- Are family members permitted to work for the company or not?
- How much do the staff socialize?

Now what?

The answers to these questions do not form a definitive list, but they will start the ideas flowing and get you looking for the right sort of information. Once you have this down on paper, you will start to get an idea of the company values and where the focus really is.

This is only the beginning – it is a very enlightened employee who is able to relate what they do in their job to what the company is trying to achieve. You are going to have to do some homework in order to persuade your staff to take ownership of the outcomes your department needs.

What has all this got to do with my department?

Quite simply, your department has some input into the achievement of the company's objectives or you would be out of a job. Your staff are the means to achieve your department's goals. If they don't know what they are trying to achieve – specifically – don't expect positive results.

How do I explain that to them – most won't understand how a business objective relates to their job?

First, look at what you have to work with. If it is only a short mission statement, you may still have to do the above research to help you clarify exactly what the company is trying to achieve. If the mission statement is detailed, that may be enough to work from.

Second, look at your department in relation to the corporate objectives. You may not have much or any input on some objectives, whilst others may be almost totally your department's responsibility to achieve. List the outcomes to which your department contributes.

Third, break down these overall departmental goals so you can identify what each individual in your department contributes. At this point it may be interesting to examine what else they do and ask yourself why they do things that do not contribute to the company objectives. There may be a very good answer, but, if there isn't, you might want to question the need to continue carrying out tasks that don't have an identifiable purpose.

I know all that – so how will this make them work any harder?

You are now in a position to discuss each person's role in the organization. This is something very few managers do. Most managers issue a job description or competency framework to staff when they start in a new job. Some managers explain what their colleagues do and how they contribute to the results of other members of staff. Few managers try to explain the big picture to their staff.

Can you imagine trying to fit a piece of jigsaw into a puzzle when you have no idea what the rest of the picture is?

The sales pitch – what's in it for ME?

If you break down everyone's job so it can be related to the company objectives:

- ◆ You will have the framework for a good performance management system which will have long-term implications for you as a high performing manager.
- ◆ You will have identified activities that are unnecessary and, therefore, can use that time to achieve more useful outcomes (more brownie points when your productivity levels rise).
- ◆ You will be better informed than the majority of other managers in the organization and can use this information effectively in management meetings to ensure focus on the most important issues (even more brownie points for being aware of critical issues).
- ◆ Your staff will be more motivated if they can see that what they are trying to achieve has some clear purpose.
- ◆ Your staff will be able to develop solutions more effectively if they know how their activities affect the big picture.

There will be more benefits for you personally – think about how much better you will be able to operate with this degree of focus.

Reflection points

Think about a time when you were given a task to do but not given a reason for doing it. This may have been at work or at home – it may even have been when you were a child.

◆ What was your immediate reaction on being told to carry out this task?
◆ How eager were you to get started?
◆ How easy was it to find a reason for not doing the task or leaving it until 'later'?

Now think of a time when you met someone who was able to explain to you their ideas in colourful detail so you could actually 'see' the outcome. How excited did you get about their ideas and how much did you want to be part of the team to make this happen?

If you could do the same for your staff, what would be the difference in their approach to what needs to be done?

Action points

Take a jigsaw with just 30 to 50 pieces. Turn the pieces face down and ensure the picture on the box is not visible. Either test yourself first or ask your team to complete the puzzle with the pieces face down. Time them with a stop watch.

Break the puzzle up and turn it face up. Allow the team to look at the picture on the box and ask them to assemble the puzzle in the normal way. Check the time taken.

Almost certainly, it will take them much longer to complete the plain puzzle than the one with the picture.

The pieces are the same shapes, the number of pieces is the same, the available reasoning power is the same. They know what they are trying to achieve – a completed puzzle – so why does it take longer when they can't see the picture?

This is a good demonstration of how difficult it is to achieve successful outcomes without a clear idea of what you are trying to achieve.

Chapter 5

The Individual

In this Chapter:

◆ **active job descriptions – what works for you and your staff**
◆ **identifying and describing the ideal candidate**
◆ **looking at alternative job descriptions**
◆ **dealing with errors.**

What the individual needs to know about their job

This may seem obvious, but how many people do you know – outside your own organization – who don't have an outline of the expectations of their role? This might be described in a number of ways – a job description, a role profile, a set of competencies – and it may be written down or verbal. For the purposes of simplicity we will refer to this as a job description.

A job description may come in many forms:

◆ It might be a list of tasks to be undertaken.
◆ It may be a list of outcomes required.
◆ It may include responsibilities and budgetary requirements.

- ◆ It may show the knowledge and skills levels required.
- ◆ It may be expressed as a series of competencies at varying levels.

It may be any or all of these – how it is expressed is not important. But the fact that there is some means of describing to the person doing the job what is expected of them *is* important.

> 'If you don't know where you are going, any road will get you there.'

Job descriptions should be recorded in some way, to ensure that the 'Chinese Whispers' effect doesn't kick in – this is when information is passed on verbally and is altered each time it is repeated, often turning into something quite different from the original. The outcome is generally 'but Fred told me to do this' and a series of blame statements ensues.

The secret of a good job description is that it works for you and for your staff. This means that it is something everyone can work with – not a complicated system. Systems developed by external experts (that may be out of date soon after they have left the organization), systems imported from other organizations and systems with many pages of information, should all be examined carefully to ensure that they do the job required of them. Most don't!

The key thing is to keep it simple. If I had to make a recommendation, I would suggest that a list of the outcomes expected of the individual's role is probably the most effective job description.

◆ A 'to do' list approach focuses on tasks, not on what the task is intended to achieve. This makes it much harder for that individual to understand *why* they are doing it.

◆ A competency framework can be effective, but takes considerable time and expertise to develop and goes out of date quite quickly. Keeping it up to date can be quite expensive.

◆ A profile of the role can be fairly complex with many different elements.

All these devices work in different circumstances. If your organization already has them and they work, use what you have, don't reinvent the wheel – but *do* use them. They are not something to be left in each employee's personal file and forgotten about.

A good job description is written down and can be updated, adjusted or otherwise developed if required. However, this should always be in discussion with the jobholder and with their agreement.

If you don't have anything to start with, examine each role in your department and decide what the key outcomes are – and prioritize them. Discuss them with the current jobholder and establish whether they are being met or if the jobholder needs some help to be able to meet them. A good place to start is often to get the jobholder to write down what *they* think the key outcomes of their role are.

Don't make the mistake of taking this at face value. The outcomes being achieved by the current jobholder may not necessarily be a good job description. There is often a gap between desired and actual performance. There is nothing wrong with this – it just means that a training need has been identified.

The first step in creating a job description for a new member of staff is to ask yourself 'Why do we need to employ someone to do this?' Perhaps it is worth considering what would happen if you *didn't* employ anyone in this role; if the answer is 'nothing' you might need to re-examine the need for another member of staff.

A good job description will make recruitment and appraisal much easier and more objective.

The ideal candidate

Write a 'person specification' describing what the ideal candidate for the job 'looks' like. In other words, what behaviours, abilities and attributes will they need?

Many job descriptions have the person specification built into them – the key areas of knowledge, skills and aptitudes. These may be expressed in terms of qualifications and experience, but there are other elements that may be of importance to a particular role.

Let's look at a few key areas:

◆ **Qualifications** – these may be educational or vocational or both.

◆ **Experience** – this should give you an idea of the build up of skills in certain areas. However, be careful – there is an old cliché that advises that you check if five years' experience means five years' experience or one year of experience repeated five times! The only way to check this out will be during the interview.

◆ **Intelligence** – harder to check on, but this usually becomes apparent at interview as you see how people respond to questions that require problem solving and creative thinking.

◆ **Physical abilities** – some jobs require certain fitness levels. Others, such as customer contact roles, need the individual to demonstrate an awareness of their personal presentation. In this category it may be stated if the job is suitable for a person with disabilities, and with what level of disability.

◆ **Interpersonal skills** – this covers social skills and the impact that the individual makes on others. If the role involves lots of teamwork, some types of people may disrupt the team or find themselves at a disadvantage in the current team environment. It isn't just a case of 'can they do the job?' on a task basis, but 'can they work with the existing people?'

◆ **Special aptitudes and interests** – any key skills or interests that might be useful for either now or the future, such as manual dexterity, or outside interests that demonstrate additional skills – perhaps chairing a local group or working with community support groups.

◆ **Personal circumstances** – always a touchy area, but there is no point in offering a job to someone who is unable to undertake the travel requirements or who is unwilling to move if the job is likely to require this.

A good person specification will not only describe the essential characteristics of the ideal candidate, but will also include additional characteristics that are desirable. For instance, it might state:

Essential – A-Level education
Desirable – English and sociology preferred subjects.

This would mean that anyone with an A level education would get through the screening process (providing all the other criteria were met), but if they had A level passes in English and sociology they would be at the top of the interview list. If many candidates have the essential qualifications, this may be an additional means of reducing the interviewing to those who have the desirable qualifications – or at least, inviting them to be interviewed first.

With a good job description and a clear person specification, it is much easier to identify the key elements of a job advertisement or a briefing document for whoever will carry out the recruitment process. It also makes screening applicants easier and results in interviews taking place only with potentially suitable candidates – which is more effective use of expensive management time than interviewing everyone who applies.

Outcomes versus tasks

There is a big difference in the results that are achieved by people focusing on outcomes compared to those who are merely concentrating on tasks. These results include not only the outcomes achieved from an individual's work, but also their attitude, level of motivation and job satisfaction.

Someone who is task oriented will work through the list of things to do, but usually has lower levels of job satisfaction because they can't see where their labours are taking them. If you can't see what happens as a result of your work, you don't appreciate the value of what you do, and it can be quite demotivating.

Being task oriented often means that there is no flexibility in what you do – you are often pinned down to the established process. If you give people a required outcome and leave the means of getting there to them, they immediately feel they have some decision-making power, and are often inclined to be more creative about the route they take to achieve the desired outcomes.

Whilst there is nothing wrong with having established processes – in some types of work they are essential – there is also nothing wrong with encouraging people to ask 'Is this the best way to do this job?' Beware of the 'if it ain't broke, don't fix it' syndrome. If you don't continuously review the potential for improved ways of working, nothing will ever get any better. If you aren't moving forwards you will find everyone else has passed you!

Having said this, some people will be scared to death if they suddenly get given carte blanche to do things their way. Decision-making power can be very scary – or it can go to some people's heads. Take things a step at a time and prepare people for a different approach. Involve them in the decision-making process a bit at a time, before allowing them free rein. Not only will this build up their confidence step by step, it also reassures you that they won't go off and do something unexpected without having thought it through carefully first.

Problem management

Everyone is human so you can expect that there will be the odd problem to deal with. The key to retaining your staff's respect and confidence is to focus on the professional, not the personal. Refer to the job description and compare what outcomes should have been achieved with what actually happened. Ask the individual to assess what went off track.

People should be allowed to make mistakes – they learn more this way. The real problem occurs when they keep making the same mistake! However, with a supportive manager and clear outlines of what is expected, repetitive mistakes are likely to be few.

The sales pitch – what's in it for ME?

If each member of your staff has a clear job description, you have a description of the ideal candidate for a new position and your team are outcome oriented, you will find that:

◆ Better quality candidates will be easily identified, so less of your time will be spent reading application forms.
◆ Less time will be spent on recruiting and interviewing, which takes you away from your key work.
◆ Closer fits between jobs and jobholders will make your department more effective.

- Individuals will be much more self-motivated.
- People will have a vision of where they are going and, therefore, are much more likely to get there.
- You will need to do less direction on a task-by-task basis.
- Your team will be more innovative and creative.
- Development needs will be clear – and, therefore, it will be easier to ensure people will acquire the needed skills (rather than a vague feeling that they aren't up to it).
- Individuals will be more able to come up with creative solutions when faced with problems.
- Higher levels of job satisfaction will be created.
- You will have more time to get on with the things only you can do – secure in the knowledge that your staff know what they are doing.

Reflection points

You have a conscientious team of hard workers who have got used to working with each other over a period of several years. They are conservative in outlook and have established processes and systems that work for them. You are looking for a new member of the group to add creative input and perhaps to encourage your valuable team to look in new directions. You have a choice of three equally experienced candidates:

◆ Candidate one is much younger than the existing team, is bubbly, bright and very creative. She has a background of working with a team of equally young creative people and is keen to change things for the better as quickly as possible. She is full of life and thinks work should be fun.

◆ Candidate two is quiet, seems introverted and has been used to working in a relatively 'lone ranger' environment and has had a fairly high level of autonomy. Older than the other two candidates, more of an age with your current team, he has demonstrated some impressive creative projects in his previous positions.

◆ Candidate three is also younger than the existing team, and has an outgoing personality, but a very business-like attitude. She has a good systematic approach to problem solving and a keen awareness of team working. Some exciting ideas have shown up in previous job history, but have been attributed to 'the team' by this candidate.

What would be the effect of hiring each of these candidates on your existing team as described above? Would this be beneficial or detrimental to your department?

Action points

If you have existing job descriptions, rewrite them as a series of prioritized outcomes. If no job descriptions exist, take this opportunity to develop the appropriate documents for each of your team. Describe the ideal candidate for each role and then compare the current jobholder with this description.

This will give you a list of development needs and the basis for a great constructive conversation with each of your team.

Chapter 6

The Horse

In this Chapter:

- ◆ **mental change processes**
- ◆ **dealing with resistance to change**
- ◆ **the steps to managing successful change.**

Change is constant

Any business that is not constantly changing is likely to fail in the not-too-distant future. With new technology, the world has shrunk to tiny proportions. We can chat to people instantly in countries thousands of miles away, work in virtual teams that are based in several different countries and know about things almost as soon as they occur, even though they may happen in different places, different time-scales and in different working environments. The outcome of all this is that if your organization doesn't move forwards it is quickly going to be passed by your competitors, who are all desperately running to keep up with the market leaders.

If you can't manage and allow for change, you're dead!

Unfortunately, human beings are not quick to embrace change; we all protect our comfort zones enthusiastically.

This behaviour happens at all levels and does not confine itself to the junior members of staff. If you are present when the newest member of the Board of Directors turns up for his first board meeting and, unwittingly sits in the chairman's habitual seat, you'll see what I mean!

Old habits die hard

No matter how keen someone is to tell you how willing they are to look for new ways of doing things, they will still have to put in considerable effort to establish a change from their usual *modus operandi*. Willingness to change and ability to change easily are not the same thing.

Change means breaking a habit – and this is difficult because habits are unconscious actions, as we saw in Chapter 2. Anything you have learned to do over a period of time has become a habit. It may be a good habit (cleaning your teeth after a meal) or a bad habit (smoking a cigarette after a meal), but you can do it without thinking about the actions required to carry it out.

Change usually requires you to 'break' an old habit and replace it with the new one. Most of us can accept this concept, but find the consequences of trying to change either irritating or frustrating when our subconscious tries to do things the old way.

The Horse

The Horse is the name that we'll give to our 'habit centre' or, to give it its correct medical name, the thymic region. This is an area in your brain that remembers all your habits – a part of your subconscious.

As we have seen, there is conscious activity and subconscious activity – in other words, things you know about at the time you are thinking them, and things that you do without consciously thinking about them at all. Anything new usually figures in your conscious mind, at least for a while. We call the thymic region 'the Horse' because it is trained in the same way as you train a horse.

If you owned a riding school and bought a new untrained horse, you would need to train it to a level where you could put a novice on its back and it would reliably circle the riding school with little input needed from the rider. This is achieved by taking the horse along the required route over and over again, until it can almost do it in its sleep. In other words, repetition, persistence and determination are required to arrive at this point. These are the same attributes that are applied when learning a new habit.

The first time you picked up a spoon as a baby, you needed lots of help and guidance to get it from the plate to your mouth reliably. The motivation was there – if you failed, you went hungry!

- ◆ Determination was required to keep trying.
- ◆ Persistence was needed to succeed.
- ◆ Repetition was needed to ensure that the activity was 'stored' by your subconscious.

The same applied when you learned to drive or operate any piece of machinery. You first needed to think about every move you made, until you had done it so often it became an unconscious action.

Discomfort zones

The first problem is that the Horse learns bad habits as easily as good ones – or we would never learn to do things that are dangerous or hazardous to our health – such as not indicating when we pull out or smoking cigarettes.

The second problem is that the Horse protects its comfort zones.

If you were riding a trained horse as a novice, you would probably find that it just followed the one in front around the riding school. It would take considerable effort and some skill to persuade it to take a different route to the other horses. You could use the reins and stirrups to give the appropriate signals and it would probably go where you asked it – until you stopped giving it the signals, at which point it would quickly return to following the other horses.

When you change from doing something in the usual way to doing it in a new way, you have to stop using automatic pilot (the Horse) and start thinking consciously about what you are doing. This can be a frustrating experience, as you have to remember to stop and think before taking action. Just move your waste bin to a different place and you will soon see what I mean.

Disputing with your Horse

What usually happens is that the Horse tries to convince you of why you should not yet make the change.

I know this sounds as though the Horse is a separate personality, but we all have conversations with ourselves, either inside our heads or, sometimes, out loud. It is not a sign of madness, more a reasoning process where we examine two aspects of something.

Let's take the waste bin situation. You have moved this from the right-hand side of your desk to the left. These are some of the rational reasons your Horse may come up with to restore the bin to its original position:

- ◆ The cleaner will move it back anyway.
- ◆ It takes too long to remember where it is.
- ◆ Somebody will trip over it in the new position.
- ◆ Other people have got used to it being there and won't like it in its new position.
- ◆ I have to stop work every time I use it because I have to remember where it is.

Part of the problem is that you have no real reason to move it – other than as an experiment. However, if you would fail a health and safety check if you left it in its original position, you would probably be more inclined to try to get used to the new position. It would not stop your frustration level each time you threw paper in the previous location, but you would persevere and, eventually, your Horse would learn the new habit.

The secret of successful change is to dispute with your Horse – and win!

This is what anyone trying to change goes through. Your job as a manager is to provide sufficient motivation, benefits, preparation and support to ensure that the process is not too painful.

The steps towards change

◆ **Purpose** – the first thing to do is to explain, in detail, why the change is important. We're back to understanding the big picture, creating a higher level of willingness to try.

◆ **Benefits** – make sure the individual knows what they will experience in the way of benefits if they successfully move forwards towards the required change (this is also known as motivation!).

◆ **Pain** – some people respond to things they will move away from as well as benefits. This means you need to make it clear what the penalties of failing to make the necessary changes would be.

◆ **Reinforcement of the benefits** – if you have to talk about the negative side of the change process, make sure you revisit the positive side before moving on.

◆ **Involvement** – ask the person who will need to make the changes what they think they will be able to do, get them to set a time-scale and help them to agree the steps they will take towards making it work.

◆ **Support** – catch them doing it right and tell them that you have noticed and appreciated their efforts. This is much more effective than waiting until they get it wrong.

◆ **Problem solving** – if they do suffer a lapse, discuss it, find out where the problem occurred and offer support in helping them to get back on track.

◆ **Praise** – give praise for their success. We all respond to praise – it makes us want to do more of whatever led to our being praised.

Help your staff to control their Horses, give them all the support you can and you will see some surprising successes.

The sales pitch – what's in it for ME?

If you know how the change process works and what your staff will experience in going through this process, you will:

- Be able to prepare people for change so that they have a higher chance of success.
- Be able to offer appropriate support so that they don't go off track or don't go far before you help them get back to where they need to be.
- Enable the department to move forwards more effectively.
- Create a supportive environment that helps your staff feel secure.
- Develop motivation that grows from successes achieved.
- Short-circuit the downward spiral that failures can create.
- Have a satisfying record of successes both individually and as a team.

Reflection points

How do you currently answer the phone?

- If you use your name, what would happen if you had to change it?
- If you say 'hello', how long would it take you to say 'good morning' reliably?
- If you answer with your department, what would happen if you moved to another department?

◆ If you answer with the company name, how would you deal with a merger that changed it to something else?

◆ During this change process, how often would you get it wrong?

◆ How would you feel each time you had to stop and remember what to say?

◆ What strategies would you use to ensure you succeeded?

Action points

◆ Take your watch off and wear it on the other wrist for a day.

◆ Notice how often you look at the wrist you usually wear it on.

◆ Note the feelings you have when you look and it's not there.

◆ Note how often you say to yourself, 'This is stupid, it's not serving any purpose, I can put it back on the other wrist now.'

Consider how your staff might use similar arguments if the purpose is not clear enough for making the change. You should be able to understand the irritation and frustration that your staff are likely to experience when dealing with change.

Chapter 7

Assessing Performance

In this Chapter:

◆ **the purpose of appraisal**

◆ **the tools to measure success, and alternative methods**

◆ **using appraisal to move forwards, not to relive the past**

◆ **preparation – gathering information and structuring appraisals**

◆ **the appraiser and appraisee relationship.**

Why is appraisal so hard?

A manager may be reluctant to carry out an appraisal for many reasons:

◆ too much paperwork involved

◆ reluctance to judge other people

◆ discomfort about giving feedback on poor performance

◆ poor time management.

I'm sure you can think of lots more reasons *not* to carry out appraisals!

Most appraisal or assessment processes are paper-based and many are so complex that the manager responsible for carrying out personal appraisals is reluctant to tackle the paper mountain and keeps the forms in the pending tray until they become urgent.

There is nothing wrong with paper-based systems, providing they have been developed with the users in mind and address the needs of the organization. Unfortunately, this is frequently *not* the case.

Appraisal systems are often imported from elsewhere – another company or someone who has a system they've used before that worked ten years ago. Sometimes a human resources 'expert' develops a system in-house, but often without discussing who will be using it, what they want from it or how much time they are willing to spend using it. Sometimes old and outdated systems have little connection with what is going on in the organization today and are virtually useless. If the organization you work for requires you to complete an annual appraisal form, then do it – but make sure the outcome benefits both the appraisee and your department and is not merely a form filling exercise. Think about how the system might be changed to suit the users better and make some suggestions. Better still, get other managers on board and get a system working for you instead of you working for the system!

The purpose of appraisal

Despite many employees' suspicions, appraisal is not meant to be a weapon to hold over the heads of the staff! A good appraisal system should be designed to establish the employee's current situation with regard to skills, knowledge, attitudes and aptitudes and then use this information to work out how to move forwards.

Appraisal should be a motivational tool; it should contribute to job satisfaction and should offer the employee a means of improving themselves and developing higher level, or new, skills.

The tools to work with

An annual paper-based assessment is not going to be enough to achieve consistent and long-term results. Appraisal should be a rolling process, ongoing and flexible, able to adapt to the needs of those who use it, both manager and employee.

Appraisal should *not*:

◆ be destructive
◆ involve any surprises
◆ be a means of handing out praise for anything that took place more than 24 hours ago (by all means mention particular instances of special effort, but praise should be given at the time the effort was made)

- be a platform for criticism of activities that no longer occur
- provide a forum for discussing other people's shortcomings.

Although your organization may carry out a periodic (annual, six monthly or quarterly) formal exercise, a good manager will conduct a continuous appraisal process on an informal basis. Individual feedback should be given as each employee tackles different tasks and develops new or improved skills. This should be part of the culture of the department – feedback, praise, problem solving, help offered freely and constructively.

So what do you need in order to carry out a good appraisal?

Let's start with the job description or role profile. If your employee has no clear idea of what they are supposed to be achieving, the appraisal process can easily turn into a conversation along these lines:

> 'You never complete the figures for the end of month petty cash outgoings for the department.'
> 'I didn't know I was supposed to.'
> 'You must do, it's always been part of your job.'
> 'Well, nobody has ever told me that.'

If there is no written job description it is impossible to argue this successfully.

It doesn't matter whether the job description is a list of tasks to do, a description of a set of competencies, a role profile with several different elements, a list of outcomes expected of the role or any combination of these. As long as something clearly describes the expectations of the jobholder, everyone will know where they are. Once both of you know what *should* be happening you can start to discuss what actually is.

You also need:

◆ an open mind
◆ a set of goals, i.e. what you want to achieve from the appraisal (and this should be on both sides)
◆ a quiet place with no interruptions
◆ some supporting facts and evidence for the issues you want to discuss.

Looking into the past or predicting the future

Many people see appraisal as an opportunity to haul out all the misdemeanours and disasters of the past year. Some managers save up their 'well dones' for the annual appraisal as well. Neither of these are useful exercises. Both errors and excellence should be tackled at the time they occur. If errors are not corrected they will continue to occur – why wait for several months before sorting a problem out? If someone does well in January, praise in July has little value.

The only useful part of looking at what has happened is to comment on whether or not progress has been made since the last time this employee discussed their performance with you.

Nor should appraisal be an exercise in setting ambitious targets without any support. Once current performance and desired performance have been established, there will either be a good match, or a gap. If there is a gap, the future needs to be discussed only in so far as to work out how this gap might be bridged by the employee and the manager together. This is not the point at which you abandon the employee with, 'OK Sunshine – there's your destination, off you go. Let me know when you get there.'

The manager's job is to help to work out the route and to provide useful advice on timetables and means of transport along the way, as well as some feedback on how the agreed schedule is progressing – a sort of tour guide.

Preparing the ground

Before sitting down to carry out an appraisal meeting, there are many things that need to be done to make things easier for both parties.

◆ Give plenty of advance warning – don't spring the appraisal on someone without allowing them time to prepare.

- If possible, let them have the format you normally use ahead of time and ask them to self-appraise.
- Carry out your own appraisal before reading their self-appraisal, but try to compare the two before you meet so you'll be able to establish all the discussion points ahead of time.
- Book a room where you will both be comfortable and there will be no interruptions.
- Do your homework – read everything you have, review the last appraisal, collect your supporting facts and evidence and have your discussion points listed.

Facts and evidence

A word about facts and evidence – they are essential to carry out a fair and balanced appraisal. If you go into an appraisal meeting with gut feelings and no substantiating facts, your credibility will drop to zero and the employee's compliance levels will be low.

Facts and evidence allow you to focus on the outcomes achieved. They also support your case and make it easy for the employee to see that you have a clear issue to discuss.

Remember that the key to a good appraisal is to focus on what happened, not on the person. For example, if Tim is consistently 15 to 20 minutes late there are a number of ways of opening the discussion regarding this.

1. 'Why can't you get up in time to get to work for 9?'
2. 'What prevents you from arriving at work on time?'
3. 'Are you aware that when you are late, other people have to interrupt their work to answer your phone calls?'
4. 'On Monday, Tuesday and Thursday of last week, Jim had to stop what he was doing to answer your phone, because you hadn't arrived in the office on time. On Tuesday this caused him to have to redo the chart he had been concentrating on, which wasted almost half an hour of his time. On Thursday he was in discussion with Gary from Marketing and me and we had to wait for him to come back before the discussion could continue. I'm sure you appreciate that this is not good practice in the overall running of the department. What do you think you can do to deal with this situation?'

It's easy to see that these are progressively more likely to result in productive outcomes. Number 1 may result in either a defensive or aggressive response. Number 2 can lead into sticky personal issues that should not be part of an appraisal. Number 3 doesn't really offer any concrete evidence and can easily be brushed off with 'well, everyone is late sometimes.' Number 4 provides facts and evidence and doesn't focus on personal issues, only on outcomes.

This sort of approach doesn't usually happen by accident – it takes forethought and planning. Prepare your questions in advance and give plenty of thought to how you will phrase them. Take notes in with you so you don't forget anything, and give the employee an opportunity to put forward their thoughts on the issue.

Roles in appraisal meetings

The manager's role in an appraisal meeting is not to talk *at* the employee. The employee should do at least 50% of the talking (ideally nearer to 70%) and the meeting should be seen as a discussion process. Consider the following:

◆ Appraisal is a collaborative means of getting from A to B.
◆ It should be 'done with', not 'done to' an employee.
◆ It should be rational not emotional.
◆ The manager is there to facilitate the process not to dictate.
◆ The employee is there to clarify what is expected of them and to get help and support in achieving these expectations.
◆ Questions are more likely to get you to a useful outcome than accusations.
◆ Difficult issues should be tackled (or they will remain difficult issues), but should focus on outcomes not personality traits.
◆ If there is a personality clash between the manager who is carrying out an appraisal and the employee

who is being appraised, it may make an appraisal meeting difficult. Ideally, any manager should be sufficiently professional to put aside personal issues, but not every employee will be able or willing to respond in the same way. A solution may be to have someone else present, or in some circumstances to have them carry out the appraisal alongside the manager concerned. This would usually be the manager's immediate superior or, occasionally, the manager's deputy.

An appraisal should be a positive and productive experience for both parties.

The sales pitch – what's in it for ME?

There is a view that the appraisal is to let the employee know how they are doing. This is true, but there is much more to it than that. If you practise ongoing appraisal for all your staff, you can expect some benefits as well.

◆ People will be more motivated and, therefore, more willing to do things to help you achieve the results your department needs.
◆ Job satisfaction will rise so you will keep those staff you've spent time developing and training.
◆ You will be able to hand over more tasks as people develop to take on more responsibility, leaving you

free to concentrate on doing those things that only you can do (like working out how to get promoted!).

◆ You won't have ongoing problems with errors continuing to occur.

◆ Your team will want to develop their skills rather than spending all their time working out how to stay out of the firing line.

◆ You will have far fewer personality clashes and personal issues to deal with.

Reflection points

◆ Think of a time when you were given a task to do with no information on how to do it, nor materials that may have been available. How did you feel about starting work on the task at that time?

◆ Think about a time when someone outlined clearly a result that was required in terms that were measurable and specific. How did you feel about getting started on this?

◆ Was the first or second experience more satisfying or motivating? Why?

Action points

◆ Identify a member of staff and describe (on paper) their current behaviour relating to a skill or job requirement. Use terms that have measurable elements and give details.

◆ For the same person and the same set of skills or requirements, write a description of what an improvement in performance would look like – what would they be saying, doing, producing, that they are not currently.

Chapter 8

Joint Ownership

In this Chapter:

◆ **establishing common ground**

◆ **offering involvement in outcomes**

◆ **helping staff to agree and focus on their own objectives**

◆ **allowing your staff the freedom to succeed.**

Whose playing field are we on?

There are many views on this one! The MD may think that they are in charge of the game, but some managers feel that their department or division is their empire and, therefore, they call the shots and decide what the outcomes should be for their bit of the organization. Some supervisors much lower down the ladder have similar ideas and, once established, won't change the way things are done – no matter what. There is the odd enlightened person who thinks that the playing field belongs to the customer.

If people don't take into account the bigger picture and think about how their activities affect the organizational goals, there is likely to be conflict. This will not only affect those in the department or section, but will affect interdepartmental relationships and, in the long term, the profitability of the entire organization. We've already looked at these issues to some extent in Chapter 4, but now we need to work out how to get that co-operation – vital to success – all the way from section to organizational level.

Getting co-operation

Most managers can get their staff to do what needs to be done one way or another through persuasion and incentives. The problem is getting them to see that things need to be done and to commit themselves to doing whatever it takes.

> It's not what happens when you are there that matters – what makes the difference is what happens when you are NOT there.

This saying is a comment on the fact that fear usually get results – as long as you're there to enforce whatever threats or bribes have been made. However, the willingness factor is still missing. People are doing what they have to do in order not to get into trouble – known as the 'pain' factor, or 'away from' motivation.

The effectiveness of this is limited. Most managers don't have the time or the inclination to be constantly monitoring every move their staff make – they need to get on with more important things and be confident that their staff know what needs to be done and will get on and do it.

Good management is when your staff do the right things and get good quality outcomes whether you are there or not.

The manager's role

There is a general expectation from most staff that managers and supervisors are there to solve problems. If things go wrong, it is the manager's job to fix it. As long as this continues, staff will bring their problems to their boss for a solution to be dispensed.

To help your staff focus on solutions rather than problems, there is a very simple formula whenever someone brings you a problem to solve – ask them how they think it should be solved. At first you may get a completely blank look, or even a response along the lines of, 'You're in charge, it's your job to sort it out.' This can always be countered with the suggestion that, as they are the person working with these issues every day, their opinion on a viable solution is valuable.

It may be quite hard to get a sensible answer the first time you try this technique, but if you persist, people will start to learn that you expect them to bring you possible solutions along with problems.

This encourages staff to think about their jobs and look at the best possible way to get their jobs done. It also starts to develop an attitude of ownership of the job, the processes and the outcomes.

Self-assessment

The more involvement you can get from your staff, the higher the chance of them developing themselves and being open to suggestions from you regarding possible learning they would benefit from.

People who are able to make a difference to their own working methods and immediate surroundings are much more likely to take responsibility for their outcomes, and get much higher quality results.

How do you get your staff to assess themselves? That's easy – they need to know:

◆ what the overall objectives are for their department
◆ the specific outcomes of their job that are required
◆ deadlines
◆ quantitative or qualitative targets
◆ why the above are important.

Understanding breeds commitment – the more someone understands *why*, the more willing they become to help to get the *what*.

Using objectives to get results

We've already talked about objectives – they are key tools to success throughout the organization, from the individual level to the corporate level.

The problem with objectives is that they tend to be rather woolly, and you can't achieve something that is difficult to pin down. We'll be looking at the concept of objective setting in the next chapter. For now let's just say that when you are discussing objectives with your people, you need to ensure they are clear about the difference between what is happening now and what should be happening when they've achieved their objectives. They should be able to tell the difference – so they'll know when they have achieved their objective by something specific that they can see, hear or feel.

Objective-based development is dependent on a number of issues:

Don't

◆ try to set goals for other people without consultation
◆ wait for mistakes to happen before you get involved
◆ pick on what went wrong
◆ blame anyone and everyone – as long as it isn't you.

Do

◆ discuss what the goals ought to be with the person or team who will be responsible for their achievement
◆ listen to their views and try to incorporate as much as possible into the final agreed goal
◆ keep a weather eye open and ensure they know that they can come for help at any time

- ◆ remember, if things come unstuck, focus on what needs to happen next to improve things
- ◆ give praise where it's due and make sure it is specific to an outcome rather than general.

Letting go

In some situations the problem with ownership is not to get the staff to take ownership – much more often the difficulty lies with the manager being reluctant to let go!

With this in mind consider the following:

If you always do what you've always done, you'll always get what you've always got.

Things won't change unless the people in the situation change – not just for a day or two, but permanently. If one person changes and another doesn't, the one who doesn't will pull the other one back to the old methods of operating – especially if that person is a manager.

A good manager doesn't need to stand over their staff to ensure the job gets done. They can leave their staff to get on with it – confident of a high quality and consistent outcome. In order to arrive at this point, an essential element is required – trust. If you don't trust your staff, they will find out very quickly and act accordingly.

The sales pitch – what's in it for ME?

Why should you go to all the trouble of persuading your staff to take responsibility for their actions when it might be much easier to rule with a rod of iron?

◆ Understanding will create higher levels of commitment amongst your staff.
◆ Job satisfaction will increase so that people will stay longer and develop better skills.
◆ Creativity and innovation will increase – you can't have all the good ideas yourself!
◆ Problems will occur less frequently because your people will be thinking about what they are doing rather than doing only what they are told.
◆ You'll have time to do those things that won't get done if you have to spend all your time keeping an eye on everyone.
◆ Your own creativity level will rise – as will your output.

Reflection points

◆ How hard would *you* work for someone who you know doesn't trust you?
◆ How can you tell that you are not trusted?
◆ What actions indicate you *are* trusted?
◆ Are you demonstrating any of the negative aspects of these to your staff?

Action points

Take one outcome you would like a member of staff to achieve.

◆ List three key reasons why this is important.
◆ Outline what effect successful achievement will have on the department.
◆ Outline what effect successful achievement will have on the organization overall.
◆ List the questions you might ask to gain their interest and 'buy-in'.

Chapter 9

Goals, Aims and Objectives

In this Chapter:

◆ **objectives at work, goals in life**

◆ **developing the 'want' list**

◆ **working towards compatibility between work and personal goals.**

Work goals don't work

Setting goals is something that helps you to achieve, but if goals are set *for* someone else it requires a very smart manager to get that person to *want* to achieve them. The problem is that we are usually willing to tackle our own goals and objectives, but need some sort of motivation to get involved in someone else's goals.

This creates an immediate problem – work goals are almost always going to be 'someone else's'. They are developed from the needs of the organization and department and may not appear to have anything much to do with each individual member of staff's wants and needs. The outcome is often lukewarm enthusiasm levels – with similarly mediocre outcomes.

What are you doing with the rest of your life?

Highly motivated people know what they want from life. Most of us have some ongoing 'wish list', but few of us write it down. We 'forget' goals that were apparently important a month or two ago, but have now faded, and are often surprised when we get what we want. This is not a particularly effective way of moving through life.

If you are focused on where you are going there is a much higher likelihood of you getting there. If you can find out what your staff want, it will make it much easier to present some of the department's objectives in a format that appeals to their personal goals.

Your support for your staff's personal goals will be appreciated and will be rewarded with much higher levels of co-operation. Most of us just want someone to be interested in what we want – ask any customer who has had to suffer an offhand attitude at the hands of a bored sales assistant. When interest is shown, the response far outweighs the effort it takes to demonstrate interest.

We are all on a journey through life, and our working life accounts for a huge chunk of that. If you enjoy what you do, like the people with whom you work, get appreciated for the effort you put in, and work in a friendly and relaxed environment – would you want to leave?

Personal goal setting

The following piece of advice could easily change your life.

Take a day off, sit down and write out all the things you want from your life. This should include the following:

◆ **Career goals** – positions you would like to achieve; how you would like to develop within your company; where you would like to see yourself in two, three and five years

◆ **Personal goals** – write down everything you have ever wanted to achieve – the places that you would like to visit and everything you have always wanted out of life

◆ **Domestic and family goals** – what you would like to achieve for your family; what the family would like to do together (e.g. improved relationships, going on holidays, plans for putting children through college)

◆ **Educational goals** – your further development; courses you would like to attend; qualifications you would like to attain.

◆ **Material goals** – things you want to obtain: e.g. car, house, sporting equipment, clothes, things for the home or the office, new stereo, etc.

◆ **Physical goals** – improving your fitness, learning a new sport, attaining a particular weight or measurements, developing a skill (e.g. to be able to run 10 kilometres, lift 100kgs).

Next break each outcome down into things to do – and then do them! This is where most goal setting fails – people write down the outcomes they want to achieve and then find that this is far too big a job to tackle, lose heart and never get started. The next chapter will help you to avoid falling into this trap!

Completing this exercise is a personal achievement and should get you steaming down the right track – now what about your staff? Can you use this exercise as a development tool for your department? How can you persuade them to not only do it, but also to share it with you?

This might take some effort but, even if you can only get them to identify the key areas they are interested in or some of the work related goals, you'll be on the right track.

Congruency – finding the matches

Everyone is different – each person has different wants and needs and different aspirations. This does not mean that you have to find different jobs for everyone in your department in line with their personal preferences. The trick is to see where there are overlaps, and skills can be put to work in creative ways.

Initially you may need to be innovative about how you match personal goals to the business needs, but there is usually some area of congruence if only you can find it. Realistically, you will never be able to satisfy everyone's goals and please all the people all of the time. However, if you can offer some interesting and useful jobs that appeal to personal preferences you will be well on the way to gaining the willing co-operation of each member of your team.

Let's look at an example:

Case study

Mark is a team leader in purchasing; he is single and keen on motorbikes. His personal goals that might impact on what he does at work include learning how to build a website, getting promoted to a higher level, earning £3000 a year more, and being able to manage projects from start to finish.

As Mark's manager, these are some things you could offer Mark to help with some of his goals:

◆ Encourage him to find out about website development programmes at night school.
◆ Liaise with the IT department about adding a page to the company Intranet and ask Mark if he would like to be involved in the design and development.
◆ Or, ask if he would like to take on the design and development with an IT department person as

mentor. This would require him to establish the objectives and content, then design and create a page to meet these criteria – a project.

◆ Ask Mark to list the skills he will need to have (and at what level) to take on the next role on the 'ladder' (even if it is yours). Review with him how he might acquire these skills and offer opportunities to shadow the current jobholder (with their involvement, of course).

There may be more opportunities, depending on what Mark's current job demands are. You may have to be creative about how you can allow time during working hours for Mark to work on a project without the rest of his work suffering. However, it is almost certain that his increased enthusiasm levels will get more done in less time!

We could look at many case studies, but each manager must think about how their staff can get more job satisfaction, and work towards personal goals whilst still focusing on getting the job done.

The sales pitch – what's in it for ME?

This all looks like it might take considerable effort – there is always a mountain of work to tackle so why should you spend your very valuable time trying to come up with creative solutions for other people's personal aspirations, when they're paid to work for you anyway?

- They'll work more willingly – less time spent by you keeping an eye on them to ensure they don't slack off!
- They'll stay longer so you are not continuously training new people to do the job.
- You'll be preparing them to take on more responsibilities; additional skills and knowledge mean less work for you in the long term.
- It will encourage your own mind to work more creatively, which should improve your own problem-solving abilities in other areas.
- Your staff will like you – not an essential, but definitely a 'nice to have' quality.
- Your reputation as a great manager will spread slowly but relentlessly.

Reflection points

- If you have the choice between doing something that needs to be done, but which you don't enjoy, and something that you find interesting and a challenge, which will you do first?
- If you know that, providing you complete the routine 'must do' tasks, you can spend time on something that you are really looking forward to doing, will your work rate rise or fall?
- If someone appears to be genuinely interested in what you want and takes steps to try to help you get

there, how do you feel about them and about any requests for co-operation that they may make?

The answers to these questions may tell you something about how your staff feel about their work and their manager (you).

Action points

Ask each member of your staff to complete a SWOT (Strengths, Weaknesses, Opportunities and Threats) analysis. Ask them to list:

- **their personal strengths (what they are good at)**
- **their weaknesses (what they don't like doing or avoid or just get wrong a lot)**
- **the opportunities that exist for them – but which they haven't done anything about**
- **the things that exist outside their control that they feel may have an impact on their work or personal situation.**

Review these with them individually – they'll give you some useful pointers on how to provide job satisfaction, as well as areas where help is needed.

Chapter 10

Priorities and Action Plans

In this Chapter:

◆ **the difference between goals and tasks**

◆ **establishing levels of importance**

◆ **breaking down goals to achieve results**

◆ **creating the habit of achievement.**

You can't DO a goal

Here's a goal:

> Get to the top of Mount Everest.

To achieve this goal, you can't just get on a plane, fly to Nepal and then start walking!

Goals require thinking about – there are lots of things to think about, and then lots more things to do. This is where many people come unstuck. They have a neatly written goals list, but never seem to achieve any of them. People who use this method – writing down goals and then looking at the list from time to time – rapidly stop bothering to write things down and will tell you 'Goal setting doesn't work for me'.

The problem is that you cannot *do* a goal. It is an outcome that results from many different tasks that you *can* do. The secret is working through the list and reviewing it constantly.

If you were planning to go to Egypt on holiday with your partner and two children, you certainly wouldn't just arrive at the nearest airport and expect to get on a plane and then find somewhere to stay when you got there. You'd need to look at travel brochures, perhaps visit a couple of websites that tell you about Egypt and what you can see. You might want to talk to friends who have been there before, or to a travel agent, about health issues, climate, suitable clothes and cultural requirements. There would be a host of other things you would need to find out, so you can make decisions, plan, organize, book and go on holiday confident that you've done everything you can to ensure it's a good one.

Most people do invest quite a lot of time and effort in choosing and planning their holidays – but don't put anything like as much effort into what they do for the other 50 weeks of the year! This, in effect, means that the holiday is the very top of their priority list out of everything else that they want in life – it's top priority.

Encourage your staff to think about creating their own goals, and action plans to achieve them, and you'll be on the way to developing really motivated people.

Prioritizing

After someone has listed all their goals and before they start creating their action plans, there is a critical activity – prioritizing.

Prioritization consists of two stages:

◆ sorting
◆ assigning importance.

Sorting involves looking at all the things you want and deciding if they are really important, quite important or would be nice to have, but don't really matter that much. This is the first part of the process. What you will end up with is a list of really important things – an 'A' list – and two lists of less important things – 'B' and 'C'.

Assigning importance requires you to decide what is top of your 'A' list, and what is next, until you've got it in some sort of order. A tip on how to do this is to write each goal on a sticky note and stick one up on a blank board or piece of wall. Take the next one that comes to hand and decide if it is more or less important than the first, then place it either above or below it. Continue this with each goal – is it more or less important than the current top of the list goal? Work down the list checking it against each one until you find out where it slots in. This should produce a working order without too much confusion.

This is the sort of thing that good time managers do with their daily 'to do' lists. The secret of getting the important jobs done first is to persuade your staff to do this with their work goals as well as their personal goals.

The 'make it happen' list

Having a list is very satisfying – but it doesn't make anything happen! You need to take each goal and break it down into things to do that will get you a step towards your goal:

Goal: holiday in Egypt
To do – visit travel agents in town and get brochures
 – get family together and look at brochures
 – do an Internet search on Egypt
 – find out what family members want to do individually
 – talk to Fred and Barbara about their Nile Cruise (last year)
 – check (Internet? Travel agent?) climate, temperature, rainy season, etc.
 – check (doctor, Internet) jabs required
 – agree holiday choice with family
 – book and pay deposit
 – put away agreed amount from pay each month
 – pay balance
 – make a list of clothes, accessories, additional luggage needed
 – budget for purchases before leaving

- get travellers cheques in appropriate currency
- check passports are valid
- arrange lift to airport and collection on return
- create a packing list (check it as you pack)
- check departure terminal (and return) and check-in time
- go!

This sort of list has a couple of things missing – times/dates and who will do what. If it's on a piece of paper somewhere it's easy to mislay it. It's also likely that you might assume that one person would do one of the tasks, only to discover – too late – that the person thought someone else was doing it.

Assign deadlines and responsibilities. If several people are involved in getting a result, get them to put their own tasks into their diaries or personal organizers entered on the day they plan to do it.

If you are writing an action plan for your own goals, by all means make a master list of all the things to be done, but ensure you assign a date to complete and put this in your diary. You may have several small tasks to do over a period of time, but they are likely to take anything between a couple of minutes and an hour each – which is not overwhelming. This means there is much more chance of you arriving at your final achievement deadline with a successful outcome – rather than crying, 'But I just didn't have the 30 hours it needed to do all this!'

This type of forward planning is essential for you as a manager – if you can get your staff doing it as well, your life will be so much easier.

This type of action planning is a habit – if you start doing this with all the things that you have to achieve, you'll find it makes life much easier and gets you consistent results. Encourage your team to do it as well and they will surprise you with their increased success.

The sales pitch – what's in it for ME?

We don't do much without some payoff for ourselves at the end of it – so what's the point of all this?

◆ You get more successful outcomes with less effort.
◆ You'll be able to achieve more of the things that you want.
◆ Your staff start to achieve more, so you don't have to do the things they haven't managed to get round to doing.
◆ Success breeds success – the more you get, the easier it becomes!
◆ You'll find your reputation as a 'go-getter' increases.
◆ Your staff will catch the achievement 'bug' and start looking for more of it.

There is one down side – if you could call it that:

◆ Other people will want you to apply your techniques to their problems!

Reflection points

If you have a dream – something you've often daydreamed about but never thought possible – think of a dozen small actions you might take that would lead you towards that dream.

Most things are achievable in small steps. Is there anything on your list you couldn't do? If so, think of something simpler, or several smaller actions that might get you the same results – be creative.

Action points

Look at that dream we were thinking about – why stop there? Finish the list and do it.

If you don't have a dream, choose something on the top of your 'Important' list and break it down into tasks. Assign deadlines and, if other people will be involved, responsibilities. Transfer tasks to diary/organizer and go for it!

Chapter 11

Training

In this Chapter:

- ◆ **the importance of training**
- ◆ **why training doesn't always get the desired results**
- ◆ **alternatives to formal training**
- ◆ **managing an individual's development**.

Does training have to take place?

The answer to this is a bit like the answer to the question 'How long is a piece of string?' In other words, there isn't a straight answer. The answer is dependent on a number of factors – individual, departmental and corporate.

I suppose the obvious answer might be that, if you want your staff to improve the level of their skills and add to their knowledge, they'll need some sort of training. However, the best means of helping them to improve is not necessarily to sit them in a training room and deliver information.

It's important to consider all the factors, not least the individual's needs and preferred method of learning.

Issues such as budget and internal resources will also have an impact on the decision as to how to develop people.

Training can, of course, take many forms. The famous (or infamous) 'sitting by Nellie' technique is a form of training where the beginner sits alongside an experienced operative and learns by watching – and, eventually, copying – what the expert does. This is most common for manual tasks, but it can be used in other areas. There are many other means of adding to people's skills and knowledge, and the informed manager should consider all the options before choosing to send someone to either an in-house or external programme.

The problem with training

The problem with training is that it doesn't usually work. This may sound unlikely, in the face of overwhelming evidence that people continue to attend a multitude of training programmes over the course of their careers. Why would organizations that, in normal circumstances, have both eyes on the profit margin spend thousands of pounds, year after year, on something that doesn't add value to the organization?

Training, managed properly, can work very well indeed. However, if all the manager does is sign up a member of staff on a course, allow for them being away for the day or days required and then expect to get them back complete with a new set of skills that they can instantly put into practice – they are bound to be disappointed.

Training is not some sort of magic spell cast over the trainees in the training room. What happens there is the tip of the iceberg. If the trainee is not clear about why they are there, then there is bound to be some sort of confusion, no matter how good the trainer is.

Ask most trainers and they will confirm that most trainees respond to the question 'Why are you here?' with one of the following:

◆ 'My name was on the list.'
◆ 'My boss sent me.'
◆ 'My boss said I had to improve my............skills.'
◆ 'At appraisal we agreed my............skills needed to get better.'
◆ 'I want to be better at............'
◆ 'Someone told me this was a good course.'
◆ 'I don't know.'

The first two and the last two indicate that the trainee has no real focus. But what about those in the middle of the list – don't they imply that there is a reason for training?

Perhaps they do – but they don't tell the trainer or the trainee precisely what the outcome should be. In order to improve, we need to know how good we are now. In other words, what is the current skill level – and what does the trainee want it to be when the training has been completed?

This may seem very obvious to you, but even when people are enlightened as to what a learning objective is, they seem to have great difficulty writing one down in specific and measurable terms. If trainees turn up without clear objectives, the trainer can include the exercise of developing objectives at the beginning of the programme, but this takes time.

In the next chapter we'll be looking at what we can do to avoid this situation.

Creative means of getting a result

What are the alternatives to formal training programmes?

Let's look at some of the means of helping people to learn. These include:

- coaching by an expert
- coaching by a colleague
- project work
- work shadowing
- multi-skill development programmes
- open learning
- day release
- work rotation
- action learning groups
- mentoring.

The majority of these strategies can take place in the workplace, with the exception of day release, which entails attending a local college to learn the theory, whilst putting it into practice in the work place.

Coaching by an expert

This is where a particular skill requires expert tuition – for example, a particular computer program such as a spreadsheet. The expert needs to be someone who is competent and familiar with the program and can pass on their knowledge in a structured manner. This will probably be in a regular session with just one or two trainees. It is a good way to impart knowledge to a single trainee, or very small groups, as long as the expert understands how to train effectively.

Coaching by a colleague

This is, in effect, 'sitting by Nellie'. The colleague teaches a set of tasks or actions that contribute to producing the outcomes required of their job. This is an excellent means of teaching manual or clerical tasks and requires only basic coaching skills to be successful. This technique is less likely to be used for developing personal skills such as time management or delegation, as a competent trainer is required to really put such concepts across effectively.

Project work

This method is less training and more working it out as you go along! It provides a challenge that stretches the individual and requires them to think creatively and logically in order to work through the requirements of a project. It may require higher than usual levels of existing skills, and the individual may also need to develop new skills, to enable them to achieve a successful outcome. This is a great way for people to extend themselves, but needs a structured monitoring and support programme to ensure it is really useful as a means of development.

Work shadowing

This is a more advanced version of 'sitting by Nellie' and offers the opportunity for an individual to see how someone, usually at a higher level, operates on a day-to-day basis. It requires the person being shadowed to be reasonably skilled in coaching. They will also need to set aside time to discuss what has been happening and allow the 'shadow' to ask questions and offer observations. Problem areas to watch out for are trainees becoming bored due to having to 'hang around' whilst mundane tasks or frequent interruptions are dealt with. Also, the person being shadowed needs endless patience and an understanding of the learning process for this to be effective.

Multi-skill development programmes

As a means of developing cover for several jobs, this can be very effective. It requires each person to pass on their skills to one other and to learn the skills of that person, to allow them to cover each other's jobs. Over a period of time, people in a team may all learn each other's roles at a basic level at least. In some teams multi-skilling is an expectation. It is an excellent way to bring people in the department together and is likely to create real understanding of other people's issues. However, unless everyone goes through a coaching skills programme first, the results and process can be very inconsistent.

Open learning

This offers the trainee the freedom to choose when and what they learn. It may be a computer-based programme that they can work through alone and may be on their own work computer or in a learning centre somewhere in the workplace or at a local college. Sometimes open learning is paper-based, with the trainee working through a series of workbooks using work-based experiences to answer questions and complete exercises. Open learning is usually supported by tutors to guide and answer questions. It requires the trainee to be dedicated and willing to make the required effort on a regular basis. But the flexible timing and length of learning sessions can provide a good way for people to manage learning alongside fluctuating workloads.

Day release

Most frequently used to acquire a qualification, this offers a day or half day each week at college acquiring the theory, ideally alongside opportunities to put theory into practice at work. The formal environment suits some people, but not others. The danger of people not attending due to high workloads can mean the investment in course fees and materials may be a high cost for a variable return.

Work rotation

This happens at all levels and some companies have a policy of management rotation at regular intervals of, say, two years. This means that the manager may find themselves managing purchasing for two years and then moving on to manage the marketing department for the next two years. Ideally, work rotation does not drop people in 'at the deep end' and a good work rotation programme will ensure that there is always a resident expert to refer to. Problems are likely to occur if pressure is high, as it takes time for newly placed people to climb the learning curve. However, it does create an excellent understanding of how other parts of the business operate.

Action learning groups

With this method, a group of people come together at regular intervals to help each other solve problems and develop skills. This is usually achieved by the group asking questions of the person with a problem until they work through all the aspects of their current 'road block' and find a solution that works. It is good if everyone takes part, but there is a need to ensure that these sessions don't turn into opportunities to gossip or complain about other members of staff.

Mentoring

This is usually employed at management level to develop high flyers or young managers. The mentor is an experienced manager at a higher level, usually not in the department of the mentoree, who acts as a sounding board, advisor, guide and sometimes coach. To be really effective, the mentor must have a clear understanding of their role and be willing to give time when required.

Managing development strategies

It is often a challenge for a manager to find the time to manage each member of their team's development programme. Ideally, the team will self-manage to some extent, but getting people to the stage where they are able to do this takes time and effort, particularly if it has not been the norm in the past.

Using an appraisal process to keep development up to date is the best base to work from. However, to keep each person's development monitored it is essential that regular 'check-ins' take place and this means careful diary use by the manager to ensure that a member of the team is not left to drift.

Regular informal 'one to one's' are an ideal means of keeping up to speed – and this doesn't mean a two-hour meeting with each member of the team every month. If team members have a specific goal and a time frame for achievement, the monitoring discussions can be put in both diaries for review. There might be just a 'how is it going?' chat for ten minutes during the interim periods, with a review at the stated deadline.

As most people's objectives will vary in time-scale, this should spread meetings reasonably well over a period of time and not result in weeks where nothing except monitoring meetings takes place.

Encouraging people to come to you when help is needed is a good strategy, but beware of those who 'don't like to bother you' and will struggle on until everything comes to a grinding halt. Having either an open door policy or a daily open door time slot when people can come and talk and expect the manager to have time to listen is often a good means of dealing with potential problem areas. However, a good manager keeps their eyes and ears open and is proactive in tackling potential problems before they reach boiling point.

The sales pitch – what's in it for ME?

Merely sending people on a training programme is easy – so what's the point in spending all this time working out alternative means of learning?

◆ Over a period of time your team will become more proactive and self-managed in relation to their development needs – meaning less work for you.
◆ Everyone is different and some people respond better to different means of learning – if you want to get

the best out of each person, offer them a means of learning that suits them.

◆ You will find options such as project work, work shadowing, multi-skilling and work rotation develop wider bases of knowledge through practice rather than merely at a theory level. Better practical skills mean better results.

◆ You will have a much 'fitter' team – better able to get the results you need the department to achieve.

◆ Job satisfaction will rise – and motivation along with it.

◆ People who learn from each other develop into good teachers of the next new recruit that joins the team – leaving you free to get on with managing.

Reflection points

If a group of trainees are from different parts of an organization – or different companies altogether – how can examples of how a technique works be related to each trainee's work situation?

For instance, in an open sales training programme there may be a computer sales person, an insurance sales person, someone who sells heavy plant equipment, a bottling machine sales person, an electronics sales person and someone who sells space in a newspaper. How can one trainer offer examples at each stage of the sales process so that every trainee can say, 'Ah, that's how it will work for me'?

What would happen if the trainer used one example – how to sell a hi-fi system to a retail customer? How might the bottling machine sales person react? What would they be thinking?

Action points

Get hold of the Honey and Mumford Learning Styles questionnaire and ask each member of your team to complete it. It will give you some guidance as to the way they prefer to learn. It is available from Peter Honey Publications as part of *The Manual of Learning Styles*, or separately on CD-ROM from Psi-Press (tel: 01483 567606, website: www.psi-press.co.uk). Basically there are four learning preferences:

◆ **The activist – who wants to get on and do something now.**
◆ **The theorist – who wants to know the background and where these ideas came from before taking action.**
◆ **The reflector – who needs to think it all through before actually putting it into practice.**
◆ **The pragmatist – who will do it, but will adjust it in a way that fits their particular set of circumstances.**

Once you have a clear idea of how each person learns best, you can try to provide methods of learning that suit their preferences.

Chapter 12

Preparing for Improvement

In this Chapter:

◆ **getting focused on the need**

◆ **the elements of achievement – why, what and how**

◆ **agreeing the objectives.**

Where are we going?

Let's assume that you have been talking to your staff about developing their skills and you have identified a gap or two in skill levels. There's a training course being run in-house that covers the material that appears to bridge those gaps. Bingo! You enrol the person on the course, they attend and everything is all right. Very good in theory – unlikely in reality.

What could go wrong?

◆ The interest level of the person who is going on the programme will affect their attitude towards the training.

◆ Their understanding of the need for improvement will affect the amount of information they take on board.

- The level of detail the trainer goes into in the areas that this person particularly needs may not meet their requirements.
- The information they acquire may not have an obvious connection to their work.
- There may not be time to put into practice what they have learned, due to work loads.

What can you do about this? As this trainee's manager – lots! Let's start at the beginning.

The why

If you've followed the advice in Chapter 4, you'll already be well on the way to an answer. The information you have gathered in Chapter 9 will give you more ideas on what this encompasses. You'll need to discuss with the person who will be attending the training programme:

- Why they need to acquire additional skills in this particular area – in relation to the job.
- Why the department needs this skill to get the results they want.
- Why and how this affects the organization in the long term.
- Why doing this programme will contribute to this individual's personal goals.

That last one is important – people do take on board the needs of the organization but their own needs are what really motivate them. In other words, we are all driven by the 'what's in it for me' syndrome.

You'll have to take the time to sit down with each person separately, which may be time-consuming, but is an investment very well worth making.

The what

If you're sending someone on a course on time management, you expect them to learn about the skills of time management. However, we all have different areas that need improvements. A typical course on basic time management will include:

- creating 'to do' lists
- prioritizing
- paper management
- meeting management
- telephone management
- dealing with interruptions
- using 'down' time
- delegation.

The more advanced time management courses will cover much more, including creating time logs, linear and lateral time management, time plans and many other things. If your member of staff just needs to get organized by planning their day better, some of this may be rocket science.

People do not attend a training programme and come back and put *everything* into practice. If you're lucky, one or two things will change – the next chapter will deal with how to optimize this.

So – *what* do you need them to do most? If you can think this one through and then discuss it in a way that encourages the trainee to agree, or even suggest themselves, what the key focus for them will be from this course, you'll be onto a winner!

The how

Knowing what an individual wants to get out of the training is a major step towards success, but even the best training course cannot deliver high levels of competency in a relatively short classroom-based programme. There are a number of actions that both the trainee and you, their manager, can take to increase the effectiveness of the training.

◆ Get the trainee to write down their learning objectives.
◆ If at all possible, pass these on to the trainer prior to the course taking place.
◆ Discuss how the trainee can apply the new knowledge they will have when they return to work.
◆ Discuss and agree what opportunities there will be for them to use new skills as soon as possible, and as often as possible, after they return to work.

◆ Agree a support programme – how often you will meet to review progress and tackle any problems that may arise.

This will create joint ownership and leave the trainee little opportunity to make excuses as to why the training has not been applied. We've all heard 'I was too busy,' or 'The trainer didn't explain that very well and I didn't like to ask,' and 'I haven't had the chance to use that since I got back.' As they say, 'Use it or lose it!'

Clear objectives

A few words about learning objectives. There is nothing more frustrating for a trainer than discovering that the trainees are unclear as to what they are expected to get out of the training session. It is all very well saying 'I want to get better' – better than what? If you can't explain how good you are now and what better means to you, this statement has little meaning. Encourage your staff to produce SMART objectives – this means that their written objective should be:

◆ Specific – in detail
◆ Measurable – something that can be seen to be different in results from current performance
◆ Achievable – not too challenging as to discourage even getting started, nor too easy so that no effort is needed
◆ Relevant – has some impact on their work

◆ Time bound – there is a finish or achievement date
for the objective.

For a basic time management course, this might look
something like:

> *By the end of this month I will be completing a 'to
> do' list every morning and prioritizing all the tasks on
> it in order of importance. I will work on the number
> one priority at all times until it is completed or moved
> as far forwards as possible by my efforts.*

If, prior to the course, the trainee has not got enough
information for this level of detail, the objective might
be more like:

> *I want to have a system to ensure that I work on top
> priority work and don't get sidetracked by other tasks
> and people asking me to do less important tasks.*

Part of the post-training debrief may be to refine or
rewrite the outcome required.

Getting agreement

Getting back to the discussion you were having before
training – what happens if you have an employee who
can't see the point of learning objectives, or is apathetic
about the whole thing and is only doing it because they
think they have to?

The answer to this is QUESTIONS.

It is useless to demand co-operation or to give someone else objectives. Co-operation must be given willingly or it isn't co-operation. If you set the objectives, they're your objectives, not someone else's.

What you need is to develop the skills of advanced questioning. You will need to do even more homework and it may be quite difficult, as people who are very apathetic frequently have no idea what their goals are.

If you've outlined what the company and department is trying to achieve and are getting down to the specifics of how this person's role impacts on that, you need to start with the yes/no questions:

> Your role is to ensure that the project worksheets are ready on time for the team to start work without having to wait for them to be completed, isn't it?
> Currently, you are finding that sometimes you're unable to meet the deadlines due to workloads, aren't you?
> If this programme were to provide you with some techniques that would help you to meet those deadlines reliably, would that be useful?

Realistically, there is only one acceptable answer to each of the above questions. At this point it may be useful to introduce a 'carrot'. This is a statement that will tell the person what advantages they will experience personally if their skills improve. It might be getting less hassle from impatient team members, lower stress levels, being able to go home on time, being seen as an efficient operator and gaining respect.

In order to do this effectively, you must know which of these matters most to them. If they are notoriously thick-skinned, suggesting that less hassle is an advantage may be akin to casting your seed on stony ground! Choose something that will strike a chord with them.

The next stage is open question asking.

> What would you like to be able to do (in relation to time management) that you're having difficulty with at present?
> What do you see as the biggest problem areas for you?

... and so on. Once you've got all this information, helping the individual to create their learning objectives may come in the form of a suggestion:

> So if we said that you'd like to find a way of being able to focus on the project plans, without constant demands from other people taking you off course, that would be really helpful. Would you agree with that?
> So what do you think the key skills might be that will help you to do that?

It may sound like a slow and painful process, but it is worth spending time to get real commitment from the individual concerned. Commitment grows from interest, and the fact that you are demonstrating interest in the trainee will usually trigger a corresponding flicker of interest in them. You'll have to keep working on it – you can't treat this as a one-off – but you'll be surprised at the turnarounds you will experience, just through taking an interest in what each person does and how they're doing.

The sales pitch – what's in it for ME?

Given that this part of the process appears to take considerable time and effort there has to be a payoff for you. As with most of the steps in the process, this will include:

◆ you will develop more motivated people who start thinking for themselves and being proactive
◆ there will be higher levels of job satisfaction for everyone
◆ staff will be focused, producing results that are really needed
◆ you will gain respect and, usually liking, from your staff
◆ sooner or later the bosses will notice how effective your team is and start thinking about how they can give you something even more challenging on which you can exercise your considerable skills!

Reflection points

- What would happen if you got into your car, started the engine and drove away without having a destination in mind?
- What would happen at the first crossroads or junction?
- If you had a passenger who directed you at each turn so that you drove around for about an hour before returning home, what feelings would you have about the passenger and about the use of your time, especially if you had other things you could have been doing?

Action points

- Take the least productive or least skilled member of your team and compare current performance with desired performance.
- Make a list of the questions you will ask to engage that person's interest and encourage commitment to gaining the necessary knowledge and skills to improve.
- Discuss the situation with the person concerned and agree a development plan.

Chapter 13

After the Event . . .

In this Chapter:

◆ **why post-training support is essential**
◆ **providing the right amount of support**
◆ **supporting the successes.**

What happened?

The best that most trainees can expect on return to work from a training course is a friendly enquiry, 'How was the training then?' As long as they give a reasonably positive response no further discussion may take place.

The expectation is that they attended the course, so they'll put it into action. If they don't, it's their fault! Unfortunately, training is not a magic spell that turns the trainee into a super-achiever! Trainees are human and are subject to the same good intentions, but poor follow-through as the rest of us.

The problem is work. We have a workload to manage which is often overwhelming. It takes all our time to get through it, without having to remember the new way to do certain tasks – there just isn't time.

Is it surprising that three months later nothing has changed? How many managers have you heard complain that, although they have sent their staff on training, the effect was only temporary and they've all gone back to doing it the way they did before?

What is their conclusion? Training is a waste of time!

Debriefs, purpose and process

No manager wants to spend the departmental budget on something that appears to be a waste of time – so what can we do?

A good first step is to ensure that all trainees get a proper debrief after their training. The sooner this takes place the better – whilst the information and good intentions are fresh! Unless there is really no alternative, it should take place within two working days of the training being completed. Strike whilst the iron is hot.

What's the point of a debrief? That's easy – you as a manager should have an overview of what the general content of the programme was intended to be, but lots of other issues may have been discussed or explored, usually in response to the needs and questions of the trainees. It's useful to know what these were.

If it has been a good training programme, the trainee should have come back with an action plan – in other words 'what I'm going to do to use my learning'. If you've been able to develop learning objectives prior to the course taking place, this action plan should be geared to these. The objectives for action may need to be rewritten – you can help to ensure that the trainee is focused on work needs.

Here are some suggestions for an effective debrief:

◆ What was the most useful thing you learned on the course?
◆ How will this help you to do your job?
◆ What might the results be if you do this?
◆ What other useful things did you learn?
◆ How can you use these at work?
◆ What do you think might make putting these things into practice difficult?
◆ What would help you?
◆ What can I do to help you?

At the end of the debrief the trainee should have a clear idea of exactly what they are going to do – on a daily basis – to put their new knowledge or skills into action.

Planning success

Don't assume that the action plan will now magically happen. Even if the trainee has not asked for your support or hasn't been able to give you an answer to the last question above, you do need to agree a monitoring schedule to give them feedback and catch problem molehills before they escalate into mountains.

Get the trainee to commit to at least one regular new 'habit' and keep watching out for it. Don't encourage them to try to do everything at once. The initial enthusiasm may well make them want to rush off and change the world overnight, but once the pressures of work hit them again, they'll find they really cannot do everything and may become demoralized. They may give up and go back to whatever they were doing before because it is easier and doesn't require conscious effort.

Making it happen and helping it to happen

As the trainee's manager you can do quite a lot to help them get to grips with new techniques. Make sure that the trainee is not trying to 'do' a goal – help them to break down the outcome they're aiming for into tasks or actions that they can carry out. They are much more likely to get started with a proper action plan.

As the trainee progresses with their new skills, remember these key points:

◆ Recognize that they will have to change the way they do something – this is always uncomfortable and they will find their subconscious is very effective at finding good reasons why the change is unnecessary just yet. Give them all the support you can – don't criticize them for not getting it right. Given that it can take up to a month to establish a new habit, you may need to be extra supportive at this stage.

◆ Don't wait until things start to go adrift before you step in. Have regular monitoring points to discuss progress – good or not. During the initial stages – the first three or four weeks – this might need to be weekly or even more often in the first week or so. This is not a general 'How are you doing?' exercise, but a specific discussion about their experiences with the new skills or knowledge.

◆ Catch them doing it right! Recognize their successes, tell them you've seen the differences that they've made already and they'll try to succeed even harder. Don't speak up only when things go wrong.

◆ Be constructive not critical. If things do go wrong, tackle it as a problem solving exercise. Encourage the trainee to analyze what happened themselves and to develop their own suggested solution. Don't make sarcastic remarks or make fun of them – and don't criticize the training they've received. Everyone should be allowed to make mistakes – it is only when the same mistake is repeated frequently that you need to remind people what is expected of them.

The more you get into the habit of following these steps, the higher the chance that your staff will be willing to approach you and ask for help before things become critical. Remember – you may be the manager, but you are also one of their team.

The sales pitch – what's in it for ME?

This is pretty straightforward:

◆ You'll get staff who actually improve visibly as a result of time spent in training.

◆ Your relationship with each individual will develop to a much higher level and your understanding of their needs will improve.

◆ People will make more effort to get it right if they know they're likely to have their efforts recognized.

◆ You will become much closer to your team, enabling you to get information, see how things are shaping up and generally be 'in the know'.

◆ Training will pay off – and you'll be able to show that it has. This should ensure that you don't find your training budget gets axed when cost cutting takes place.

Reflection points

◆ If each member of your team improved one skill by 20%, what difference would it make to the output of your department?
◆ If you had to invest three hours a month in each member of your team for the first month and then

about 5 minutes a week for the next month, would it be worth the difference in output over the forthcoming year?

Note – if your team has more than about eight people in it, you need to train team leaders to take on some of the above responsibilities. This is good development for them and means less for you to do.

Action points

◆ Find the least organized person in your team and coach them in preparing a daily 'to do' list and prioritizing the tasks on it. You may have to work with them on this for the first week or so.

◆ Monitor them over two months – meet at least once a week, even if only for five to ten minutes and discuss progress. Actively look for successes and congratulate them – not just 'well done', but appreciating the result achieved.

◆ Keep a record of the total amount of time you have invested in this project.

◆ Make a record of the achievements of the person who is making the changes.

◆ At the end of the two months review the results versus your time investment.

Chapter 14

What Next?

In this Chapter:

◆ **dealing with success**

◆ **how to repeat success consistently**

◆ **using knowledge to help yourself as well as your staff**

◆ **the steps to moving up.**

What happens after success?

People often return from a training programme full of enthusiasm. If the trainer is good, they should have enjoyed the training. The more fun it was, the more they will remember of it. They will be keen to take action and the manager's role is often merely guide and cheerleader. It may take a little gentle encouragement to keep them on track when work pressures get tough, but those who are keen and have their learning objectives and action plans worked out, will have a good chance of achieving success.

So, at some point, depending on the complexity of the goals they're aiming to achieve, they will get what they were trying for. The new skills will have matured and become the 'norm' and the knowledge they've acquired will have been applied and have become something they use daily. The challenge is over – now what?

Making one development strategy work over and over again

It is rare that a training programme has only one nugget of useful information for the trainee. Usually there are lots of useful things that could be used, but it just isn't realistic to change everything at once. The secret of making training *really* pay off is to revisit the training notes with the trainee and discuss what else might be useful. Then you follow the process outlined in Chapter 13 and support them through putting another technique or skill to work. A really good programme will produce several new skills or pieces of knowledge that will make a real difference to the individual's success.

If a particular way of working is effective for one person, might it be possible for them to coach others who would benefit from this? Training doesn't work on its own – but in the hands of a good manager it pays off over and over again!

Practising what you preach

It's easy to fall into the 'do as I say, not as I do' trap. If you want to be taken seriously and retain your credibility, you must apply all these skills to your own development.

If your manager or director is not as enlightened as you are, if they don't offer you the support you need, you may have to ask for their help. No matter how motivated you are, we are all human and need some feedback and encouragement to keep us on track. Buy your boss a copy of this book and ask for what you want – you might have to find a diplomatic way of suggesting that they could be a great boss if only...

If you happen to be self-employed or don't have someone whom you could ask for this kind of help, look for a mentor. Don't be afraid to ask someone if they would be willing to give you some support – most people are flattered to be asked. Bear the following points in mind:

◆ Set out the ground rules for the relationship – what you would like from the mentor and what they feel comfortable in offering.
◆ Agree the frequency and, perhaps, the length of the meetings.
◆ Have an objective for each meeting.
◆ Don't ask your mentor to solve all your problems – their role is to provide experience and help you to solve your own problems.
◆ Do use your mentor to bounce ideas off.
◆ Do share your goals – personal and career. A mentor can't help if they don't know what you're trying to achieve.

Preparing for promotion

If you are successful in following your own advice and successful in achieving your goals, sooner or later someone will notice. Unless you are already at the top of the heap, you'll be on the fast track to promotion.

There are two types of promotion:

◆ by merit
◆ by long service.

The second only happens once or twice before the individual achieves a level that is the limit of their skills. Occasionally managers are promoted beyond their competence level, but this is inevitably a recipe for disaster and does the organization no good at all.

Promotion on merit can come two ways:

◆ Keep working hard and someone will notice eventually.
◆ Find out what you need to know to get the next job up the ladder – or a specific role you've targeted. Acquire and demonstrate the skills needed for this role, preferably to those who will be making the decision.

There is one big problem – if you're ready to move on, who will take on your responsibilities? If you've been following the techniques in this book, you should have someone trained and ready to go – so what's stopping you!

Summary

All the information in this book is good common sense but, as they say, common sense is not very common! We all know what we should be doing; we just don't do it.

We've explored the basic groundwork of attitude and approach and looked at the benefits that creating a positive environment can make to you as a manager and to your team. It will certainly focus them on what can be done rather than on the problems and setbacks. Just watching your own language to ensure it focuses on positive rather than negative messages will help create this environment. Make sure you are not preparing people for failure instead of setting the scene for success.

We have also dealt with focus and knowing where you're going. This may seem obvious – but over many years I have come across very, very few companies that actually let their people know what they're trying to do. There is often an expectation that they will just 'know', or, worse still, a belief that too much information is dangerous!

The importance of having goals and someone who will offer support throughout the change process cannot be emphasized enough. For a manager there is nothing that can be substituted for time spent gaining co-operation and ownership at the beginning. If it isn't there to start with, everything else will be a real uphill struggle and it will need far more effort to keep everything moving forwards.

In order for your staff to perform at their best they will almost certainly need to gain additional knowledge and skills. Certainly, as time passes and responsibilities grow and change, there will be a need for more information and development of existing skills. Don't just send them for someone else to force-feed information. Think about how they might best learn and use their preferences to get the best results in the shortest time.

Remember that there is a before and an after to training. Your input to this will make a real difference to the results you get – not in one or two percent terms, but in 80 and 90 percent terms!

Finally, prepare to develop yourself – be ready to move onwards and upwards and enjoy the challenges that will be yours if you really do grow your own achievers to carry on when you move up!